MIS-EDUCATION IN SCHOOLS

BEYOND THE SLOGANS AND DOUBLE-TALK

Howard Good

Rowman & Littlefield Education
Lanham • New York • Toronto • Oxford

Published in the United States of America
by Rowman & Littlefield Education
A Division of Rowman & Littlefield Publishers, Inc.
A wholly owned subsidiary of The Rowman & Littlefield Publishing Group, Inc.
4501 Forbes Boulevard, Suite 200, Lanham, Maryland 20706
www.rowmaneducation.com

PO Box 317
Oxford
OX2 9RU, UK

British Library Cataloguing in Publication Information Available

Library of Congress Cataloging-in-Publication Data

Good, Howard, 1951–
  Mis-education in schools : beyond the slogans and double-talk / Howard Good.
    p. cm.
  Includes bibliographical references.
  ISBN-13: 978-1-57886-534-5 (cloth : alk. paper)
  ISBN-10: 1-57886-534-4 (cloth : alk. paper)
  ISBN-13: 978-1-57886-535-2 (pbk : alk. paper)
  ISBN-10: 1-57886-535-2 (pbk : alk. paper)
  1. Education—Aims and objectives—United States. I. Title.
  LA217.2.G6624 2006
  370.973—dc22   2006021398

For Darla,
a little rascal

What the best and wisest parent wants for his own child that must the community want for all its children.

—John Dewey

CONTENTS

PREFACE

Choosing a title for a book is a process fraught with peril, not unlike choosing a name for your child. In both cases, a poor choice can have long-term repercussions. Just look at my name.

What were my parents thinking? Didn't they realize it was impossible to be taken seriously as a hipster—or anything else—with a nerdy name like Howard? How could they start me out in life with such a fatal handicap?

There may have been a few cool Howards—Howard Hawks (director), Howard Zinn (historian), *Howards End* (novel). But, on the whole, it's a name associated with fussbudgets and cuckolds, which is why I go by Howie most of the time.

I bring this up because *Mis-Education in Schools: Beyond the Slogans and Double-Talk* wasn't the original title of the book you're holding. The original title was *Gathering Fuel in Vacant Lots: Stories of Mis-Education*, derived from the closing lines of one of my favorite poems, T. S. Eliot's "Preludes." It was changed at the insistence of the publisher. Eliot may have been a major poet, but he apparently knew squat about modern marketing.

The new title, though it lacks poetry, still expresses my frustration as a parent, teacher, and former school board member with the vast amount of uninspired schooling going on in this country. As with the weather, everyone talks about school reform, but no one does much about it. And what is done—for example, the No Child Left Behind Act—often makes the weather where kids live worse.

Anyone who's read my three previous books on education or my essays in *Education Week*, *Teacher Magazine*, and *American School Board Journal* knows I believe that schools should free up the energies of teachers and students, not attempt to overregulate or suppress them, as routinely happens now. This makes me sound to some people like a wild-eyed anarchist with a manifesto in one hand and a lighted bomb (or joint) in the other.

But my educational philosophy is actually pretty simple and straightforward and was largely summed up by something John Dewey once said: "What the best and wisest parent wants for his own child that must the community want for all its children."[1]

I'm not the best or wisest parent and have never pretended to be—except, of course, in front of my four kids. My mom, who died while I was writing this book, came closer to the ideal.

She was my very first teacher. The stuff she taught me—how to tie my shoes, cook an omelet, read for pleasure, speak my mind— has proved more useful and durable than most of what I learned in school. She wanted my three brothers and me to grow up to be the kind of people who had high expectations for themselves and did the right thing because it was the right thing to do and could, as I mentioned, tie their own shoes.

Schools today wouldn't dare adopt this as their educational agenda, even if it meant happier kids and a better world. Why? Student test scores might suffer.

But there's more to education than testing. At least my mom would say so, and I always—well, usually (okay, sometimes)—listened to my mother.

NOTE

1. Martin S. Dworkin, ed., *Dewey on Education: Selections* (New York: Teachers College Press, 1959), 34.

1

DOING THE MATH

I was just settling down to work when, of course, the phone rang. I jumped up from my computer and dashed to the kitchen to answer it.

"Hello?"

"Howie, this is Janet Gellar."

Oh shit. Mrs. Gellar was my daughter Darla's ninth-grade math teacher. She'd taught my three older children as well. If Mrs. Gellar was calling, it wasn't because she had good news to share.

"Darla had a meltdown in class today," she said.

"What happened?" I asked, though I'd some idea. Darla had been struggling in Accelerated Math ever since school started five weeks ago.

Mrs. Gellar explained that there'd been a big math test that morning. Overwhelmed by nerves, Darla suddenly forgot the various formulas she'd studied. Then, with time running out and half the test still to do, she burst into tears.

"I felt awful," Mrs. Gellar added.

But not so awful that she didn't give Darla a 58 on the test. I sensed that she wasn't as concerned about Darla as she was about Darla's grade.

"Well," I said, "what do you suggest? It isn't like Darla's not trying."

Poor Darla was already staying after school for extra help most days and reviewing her class notes before going to sleep most nights. I'd walk past her room, and she'd be sitting up in bed staring into her notebook with an anguished expression on her heart-shaped face.

Mrs. Gellar proposed what sounded like a simple remedy—switch Darla from Accelerated Math to a regular math class that met during the same period.

"Who's the teacher?" I asked.

She told me. I sighed. It was someone with a reputation for being chronically grouchy to students.

● ● ●

Late in the summer, a letter arrived from the high school saying Darla had been placed in Accelerated Math. It wasn't something my wife and I had sought. Darla had always gotten good grades in math, but only by working incredibly hard. She never seemed to have a natural facility for the subject or even to enjoy it. None of this apparently mattered to the school. Placement had been based on teacher recommendations and her score on the state's eighth-grade math assessment.

But now, just a few weeks into the school year, Darla was in frantic need of rescue. It made me wonder exactly how reliable the placement process was. I had a hellish vision straight out of Hieronymus Bosch of thousands of high school students being tormented in hundreds of classes where they were baffled and bored and didn't belong.

It also made me wonder what a student had to do to win over a teacher. While Darla was going down, Mrs. Gellar just stood on the shore waving bye-bye.

"A student," Nel Noddings wrote, "should not have to succeed at A.P. calculus to gain a math teacher's respect."[1] There are other things besides high test scores—like motivation and effort—for which students should be recognized. People can make it in life without being able to find the angle of the hypotenuse of a triangle. But they can't make it without being able to work hard or persevere or take risks. Throughout her struggles in math, Darla exhibited all these qualities in abundance. Unfortunately, Mrs. Gellar chose, as most teachers do, to overlook or at least undervalue the importance of them.

• • •

Although Mrs. Gellar favored us switching Darla out of Accelerated Math, it was unclear whether we could. The principal, who was new, had decreed that all schedule changes had to occur within the first five days of school. "But that's crazy," I said. Mrs. Gellar assured me that it was the principal's policy nonetheless.

I decided I'd better call Darla's guidance counselor, a Mrs. Hogan, who was also new. She wasn't there, but the secretary took my name and number.

"Mrs. Hogan will get back to you."

"Today? I asked.

"Definitely," the secretary said.

I wouldn't hear from her until the following week.

• • •

Research indicates that when parents are involved in their children's education, the children achieve higher grades and test scores.[2] But what constitutes parental involvement? Serving as a room mother? Joining the PTA? Helping your children with their homework? Or can it be something more fundamental, such as having a say in the kind of place school is and the kind of values taught there?

As researchers use the term—and schools generally use it in the same sense—parental involvement doesn't mean debating a school's educational philosophy and goals. A parent who shows up at the schoolhouse door with questions or criticisms is almost guaranteed a hostile reception. I myself have felt about as welcome as a skinhead at a synagogue.

By parental involvement, most schools mean parental compliance. This can take many forms, including making sure children attend school regularly, limiting children's television watching, encouraging children to read at home, and establishing a daily family routine for homework, chores, meals, and bedtime.[3] All these activities have one thing in common. According to the latest research, they contribute to students scoring higher on tests.[4] And, under the federal No Child Left Behind Act (NCLB), mandatory testing has become the sine qua non, ne plus ultra, and Magna Carta of American education.

You'd think parents have a right to say how their children should be educated. But if parents have such a right, they don't often get to exercise it. Not even teachers have the kind of say they once did. Increasingly, they're forced to "teach to the test." The NCLB represents, as Theodore R. Sizer observed, the eclipsing of local autonomy and the imposition of one standard for all.[5] It has moved control over children's education away from the classroom teachers who know them and the parents who love them to a centralized bureaucracy that doesn't know them or love them or, quite frankly, give a damn about them as individuals.

• • •

When the school bus dropped Darla off at our driveway that afternoon, she looked on the verge of tears. She already knew that she had gotten a 58 on the test and that Mrs. Gellar had called me. I watched her walk up the driveway, my heart breaking for her. She was barely in the door before she asked what Mrs. Gellar had said. As soon as I started to tell her, the tears poured out.

"I hate math," she sobbed. "I hate it."

• • •

"Tasks that cause a student to fail because they are selected at an incorrect level of difficulty," Rob Bocchino wrote in his book, *Emotional Literacy*, "damage the student's self-esteem. . . . When a student learns to 'hate' a subject or task, he is really trying to protect his ego by avoiding the topic that 'caused' the negative feeling or by attributing his failure to the teacher or the subject itself."[6] This seems like an apt description of what was happening to Darla. Except for one thing—Darla wasn't actually failing Accelerated Math. Her overall average in the class, though not great (in the mid-70s), was still passing. If she hated math, the reason wasn't because she couldn't do it but because she'd come to feel she couldn't.

Part of why Darla felt that way was the teacher. After Mrs. Gellar handed back the test, for example, she informed the class that two students had failed. She didn't name them, but they knew who they were, and their feelings of inadequacy and shame only deepened with her public reference to their failures and the rest of the class's success. That Mrs. Gellar may have been unconscious of her cruelty doesn't make it any less hurtful or make her any less culpable. A teacher has a duty to help every student, or at least not hurt any of them.

But also undermining Darla's confidence in her math abilities was the manic pace of instruction. The concepts taught in Accelerated Math are the same as those taught in regular math but in only half the time. Is it any wonder the class has a reputation for causing stress, fatigue, and hand-wringing among even the hardiest students?

Sizer points out the "damnable problem" that "no one of us learns . . . in precisely the same period of time. . . . Some of us are 'fast' learners, in some subjects but perhaps not others, and some are 'slow.'" He recalls that as an eighth grader, he'd freeze up whenever his teacher would write a question on the board and announce, "It's quiz time! You've got ten minutes. Now, go!" Pop quizzes, he said, were a poor demonstration of what he could do. His best schoolwork "emerged from slow, time-consuming toil."[7]

Students are still being judged, compared, and sorted by how well they do on timed tests. Most schools have developed "Honors" tracks to accommodate the swift and "Regular" and "Special" tracks for the less facile.[8] There's nothing particularly scientific or objective about this sorting. Much of it follows the socioeconomic status of students' parents. In effect, the stratified society that exists outside schools has been replicated within schools.[9]

Perhaps if we were seriously interested in creating schools that operated democratically, we'd end the practice of tracking, which sends some students on to wealth and privilege but limits the future prospects of many others. "Let's put all our children in the same boat," education writer Meredith Maran urged, "then work together to raise the level of the river."[10] At the very least, let's abandon the notion that there's a fixed timetable for learning a subject and that children who learn on a different schedule are "Regular" or "Special"—ed-speak for inferior. They aren't; no child who's loved by someone ever is.

● ● ●

By Monday morning, I'd yet to hear back from Darla's guidance counselor, Mrs. Hogan. I called her again. Not there. I was starting to think I'd have to crash her office loaded on Robitussin and elderberry wine in order to get her attention. But while I was in the middle of imagining the heinous scene, the phone rang. It was she.

I described Darla's problem and told her Mrs. Gellar's proposed solution. I did it in the calm, patient tones of a mature adult who's accustomed to using reason, but I very nearly grew an instant brain tumor when she responded by citing the principal's five-day rule.

"You can't just leave Darla trapped in a class where she's struggling," I exploded. "What's the point? To make her feel like a failure? It'd be one thing if she wasn't trying or if the teacher was willing to stick with her, but that isn't the case. You've got to be fair."

Mrs. Hogan didn't answer right away. Perhaps she was thanking God that I hadn't showed up at her office in person half out of my mind from abusing cough syrup. Finally, she said, "I'll need to talk to Mr. Stevens"—the principal—"and he's not here today."

I wanted to weep, curse, scream. "Oh," was all I said.

● ● ●

As swampy as things can get at the bottom of a hierarchical system like education, it's often only an extension of an even worse swamp at the top. Just look at the recent history of math education in New York State. It has been one great slough.

In the late 1990s, the State Education Department (SED) essentially did away with local diplomas as part of its effort to "raise"—notice I put the word in quotes—academic standards. Henceforth, all but classified students would receive the more rigorous—perhaps I should put that word in quotes, too—state Regents diploma. This meant that thousands of high school students who never would've taken Course I Math or Earth Science were now required to pass Regents exams in these and other subjects.

Admittedly, the old local diplomas were of questionable value—kind of the academic equivalent of Canadian money. But the new diploma raised just as many concerns. Parents worried about their children repeatedly failing one or more of the Regents exams and being stuck in high school forever. School boards worried about the cost of having superannuated students take up class space long after they should've graduated. Teachers worried about what parents and school boards would do to them if the worst fears of both actually came true.

It wasn't enough for SED, though, that math teachers were teaching a whole new type of student. They would also have to teach a whole new type of course. SED decided to scrap Course I as of 2002, substituting Math A and Math B. The change went into effect before districts had time to adjust curriculum or replace textbooks.[11]

The results were what anyone in touch with reality might've predicted. Students flunked the Math A Regents in astonishing numbers. In some districts, the failure rate reached 100 percent.

"Oops!" doesn't quite sum it up. One study revealed that math education in the classroom had become so muddled that it no longer matched the state's standards or provided a logical progression for students. Even the names Math A and Math B were found to reflect ambiguity about which topics should be covered.[12]

Now SED is trying to bury the mess it made. Darla and her classmates will be the last students to suffer through Math A and Math B. Future students will get to suffer through Integrated Algebra and Integrated Geometry.[13]

The committee of math teachers, professors, and educational professionals that recommended the latest overhaul called on SED to pursue "a set of world-class standards, as good as any in the world."[14] What the committee neglected to mention was how difficult it would be for most students to meet such standards—ever. According to the 2003 scores from the National Assessment of Educational Progress, only 33 percent of the state's fourth graders and 32 percent of its eighth graders met a national math standard.[15]

But the larger question may be whether national or world-class standards are even worth meeting. Nel Noddings thought not.[16] "The kind of people we are turning out," she wrote, "is more important than national supremacy in mathematics and science."[17] And unless we start turning out the kind of people who know what truly counts in life, it won't much matter who wins the world title in math.

• • •

When I hadn't heard from Mrs. Hogan by lunchtime Tuesday, I phoned her. Perhaps it was a good thing she was out. It put off for another half hour a conversation that left me fuming.

"Yeah, I talked to Mr. Stevens," she told me. "He said it's too late for Darla to change from Accelerated Math. She'll get an F in the course if she drops."

I was incredulous, though I shouldn't have been. I should've known that the school would be about as responsive to parental concerns and student needs as Genghis Khan was to his captives' pleas for mercy.

"That's it?" I asked. "That's the best solution available? That she just continue to flounder?"

There was silence at the other end of the line, so I added, "You're a professional educator. Does consigning Darla to roast in math hell seem educationally sound to you?"

"I'm taking the Fifth," Mrs. Hogan said. She may have thought the principal's decision was wrong, but she wasn't going to admit it. How could she? She was new to the district and untenured.

• • •

What exactly does the term "professional educator" mean? "'Professional educator,'" the Wisconsin State Department of Public

Instruction says on its website, "means an individual who demonstrates through performance the knowledge, skills, and disposition to improve pupil learning and qualifies . . . to hold a professional educator license." The Kansas State Department of Education offers a more detailed definition, explaining with all the eloquence of a shopping list that the professional educator is "liberally educated," "assumes a professional role within the organizational system of the school," "combines an understanding of relevant academic disciplines with an appreciation for pedagogical theory and research," "respects and values all persons and provides a supportive environment for diverse learners," "integrates appropriate technology into the educational process," "demonstrates knowledge and use of multiple assessment and diagnostic techniques," and "utilizes reflection as a tool for self-growth, program assessment and instructional effectiveness."[18]

Although one definition is long and turgid and the other short and seemingly to the point, both manage to obscure the same central fact—that the professional educator, whether working in Wisconsin or Kansas or, alas, New York, is first and always an employee. And an employee has only limited autonomy. He or she is expected to do as told. The more independent and willful an employee is, the less professional he or she is actually considered to be.

The rub for professional educators is that while they are, like doctors and lawyers, professionals in name, they are, unlike doctors and lawyers, employees in fact. Their roles and responsibilities are prescribed, often down to the smallest detail, by union work rules, district policies, and state regulations. They can bend a rule here or blunt a policy there, but most are reluctant to be openly critical when criticism might bring them into conflict with power holders. To speak out risks retaliation from principals, school board members, or faculty cliques, and the risk is greatest for the untenured, who can be fired without districts having to show cause.

By retreating into a kind of frightened silence, professional educators injure not only students but also, as Maxine Greene warned, their own standing. "We who are teachers," she said, "would have to accommodate ourselves to lives as clerks or functionaries if we did not have in mind a quest for a better state of things for those we teach and for the world we all share. It is simply not enough for us to reproduce the way things are"[19]—particularly as the way things are sucks.

• • •

A couple questions suddenly occurred to me that should've occurred to me earlier. Was the five-day rule an official district policy or just something the principal had concocted? Did the school board even know the principal was enforcing it? I phoned a board member, a woman who had taught my kids piano when they were younger, to find out.

"I don't remember us ever approving anything like that," she said.

The fact that she didn't remember it might be significant or might not. I'd served six years on the school board, including three as president, and never ceased to be amazed at what some board members couldn't remember from one week to the next. Mark Twain wasn't joking—well, he was joking, but he had a serious point withal—when he remarked, "God made the Idiot for practice and then He made the School Board."

The thing for me to do was consult the Highland High School student handbook. We kept it in the kitchen junk drawer along with pens, pencil stubs, hotel notepads, loose thumbtacks, old unidentifiable keys, a lint roller, refills for the lint roller, batteries, and assembly instructions for various appliances we no longer owned.

According to the handbook's table of contents, information about "Schedule Changes" was on page 2. I turned to it and read the following:

> Any schedule changes must occur within the first five days of each new semester. . . . After five days, only teacher or administrator initiated class changes will be considered. ANY STUDENT-INITIATED CLASS CHANGE AFTER FIVE (5) DAYS OF THE SEMESTER WILL RESULT IN A GRADE OF "F" AND LOSS OF CREDIT FOR THE SEMESTER.

Despite the last sentence, with its multiple threats in capital letters, Darla could still change classes under this policy. I immediately phoned Mrs. Hogan.

"You and the principal should get yourselves copies of the school handbook," I suggested. "It says right on page 2 that teacher-initiated changes are allowed."

I read the relevant portion to her. When I finished, I pictured her collapsing in on herself like a metal folding chair.

"Let me check with a few people," she wearily said. "I'll be back to you."

While I waited, I phoned the principal, the superintendent, and the forgetful board member. None of them was in, but I left long and what I bet they thought were sarcastic messages.

• • •

In an attempt to identify the sources of student alienation, Karen Oerlemans and Heather Jenkins interviewed students who were chronically absent from their West Australia high school. The students told the researchers that they felt powerless, with little control over their choice of courses or what happened in class. Many said their interests were ignored in favor of the school's rules and policies. To them, the rules reflected the power held by teachers and school administrators. They perceived school as using the rules in a negative fashion, to enforce discipline, rather than in a positive fashion, to promote a sense of community.[20]

Similar feelings of powerlessness are common among American high school students. One educational theorist has gone so far as to say that "we are in danger of allowing our schools to become academies of alienation."[21] The high school Darla attends is fairly typical. With its rigid timetable, standardized curriculum, and petty rules about food, dress, and cell phones, it's a cross between a factory and a minimum-security prison. The school even has a uniformed police officer, a gun on his hip, patrolling the premises.

Given these conditions, you can hardly blame students for thinking the adults in the building fear and mistrust them or for resenting it. The sad part is that most students once liked school and eagerly did what teachers asked them to do. But after the early grades, the number of students who find school rewarding starts to drop significantly. William Glasser, author of *The Quality School*, said this is because "the coercion is stronger, and students do not feel nearly as good as they did in the lower grades."[22]

It isn't only people who teach. The overall atmosphere of a school teaches, too. When rules are many and oppressive, or when classes are pointless and dull, school teaches students that, in the great scheme of things, they matter least.

• • •

I never got a call back from the guidance counselor. Instead, the principal—whom the students had nicknamed "Alf" for his supposed resemblance to the furry orange alien on TV—called me.

This wasn't an easy conversation for either of us. Although he'd been principal less than a year, I had some history with him, all of it bad. The previous semester, he'd pulled my older daughter, then a senior, out of English class and threatened her with detention if she didn't inform on the combatants in a food fight she'd witnessed in the cafeteria. I was livid and let him, the superintendent, and the school board know it. Perhaps I'm unusual, but I don't send my kids to school to learn how to be a snitch.

Now he was on the phone telling me that Darla could change math classes. "Since the teacher recommended it," he said, "we'll allow it." I later heard he flew into an impotent rage when the guidance counselor pointed out to him that they'd been violating their own policy.

A happy ending? Somehow no. Looking back, I'm most struck by the fact that the school systematically betrayed Darla. There was the teacher who was in such a rush to cover material that she couldn't stop to help. There was the guidance counselor who knew something was wrong but refused to admit it or do anything about it. There was the principal who tried to enforce a rule that didn't even exist. There was the school board member who wandered around in an amnesiac haze.

Ask these people, they'd say every kid counts, but when I do the math—guess what?—it doesn't add up.

NOTES

1. Nel Noddings, *The Challenge to Care in Schools* (New York: Teachers College Press, 1992), 158.

2. "Family Involvement," http://www.dcps.com/ppp/family_readthis.htm (accessed October 28, 2004).

3. "Family Involvement."

4. "Family Involvement."

5. Theodore R. Sizer, *The Red Pencil: Convictions from Experience in Education* (New Haven, Conn.: Yale University Press, 2004), 72–73.

6. Rob Bocchino, *Emotional Literacy: To Be a Different Kind of Smart*, http://www.robandkathy.com/followup/ (accessed October 26, 2004).

7. Sizer, *The Red Pencil*, 62.

8. Sizer, *The Red Pencil*, 63.

9. Theodore R. Sizer and Nancy Faust Sizer, *The Students Are Watching* (Boston: Beacon Press, 1999), 69.

10. Meredith Maran, *Class Dismissed* (New York: St. Martin's Press, 2000), 291–92.

11. "Regents Consider Policy Changes," *New York Teacher*, November 4, 2004, 3.

12. Associated Press, "Regents Plan Math Overhaul," *Poughkeepsie* (N.Y.) *Journal*, November 5, 2004, 7A.

13. Associated Press, "Regents Plan Math Overhaul," 7A.

14. Associated Press, "Regents Plan Math Overhaul," 7A.

15. Associated Press, "Regents Plan Math Overhaul," 7A.

16. Susan Ohanian doesn't think so either. "What Standardistos"—her sardonic name for those behind the standards movement—"don't seem to grasp is, whether you're talking about national tests or corporate hierarchies, not everybody can—or wants to—be top banana. Some people will be presidents; others will be custodians. We need both. If society is to function, we need every manner of worker." *One Size Fits Few: The Folly of Education Standards* (Portsmouth, N.H.: Heinemann, 1999), 15–16.

17. Nel Noddings, *Educating Moral People: A Caring Alternative to Character Education* (New York: Teachers College Press, 2002), 129.

18. Other states' departments of education presumably have similar definitions, but these were the only two I found posted on the Web when I Googled the term "Professional Educator."

19. Maxine Greene, *Releasing the Imagination* (San Francisco: Jossey-Bass, 1995), 1.

20. K. Oerlemans and H. Jenkins, "Their Voice: Student Perceptions of the Sources of Alienation in Secondary School," *Proceedings Western Australian Institute for Educational Research Forum 1998*, http://www.waier.org.au/forums/1998/oerlemans.html (accessed April 7, 2003).

21. Urie Bronfenbrenner, "Alienation and the Four Worlds of Childhood," *Phi Delta Kappan 69* (February 1986): 436.

22. William Glasser, *The Quality School*, rev. ed. (New York: Harper, 1998), 72.

2

A SNITCH IN TIME

If they want to play high school sports, students in my district must sign a pledge not to smoke tobacco, drink alcohol, or use drugs. This may sound like a good idea to you, the kind of character-building activity more districts should pursue, but there's one big problem with it: the student athletes don't always keep their word.

An assistant football coach, the father of a close friend of Darla's, told me about a recent and rather considerable lapse. One Saturday night the fall sports teams held a party in a motel room across the river. Hulking football players drank and mingled with nimble soccer players, preppie tennis players, stoic cross-country runners, and bouncy cheerleaders. When the party started to get out of hand, spilling into the hall and parking lot, the desk clerk had second thoughts. He picked up the phone and called the police.

The motel soon resembled something out of the TV show *Cops* ("Bad boys, bad boys, what ya gonna do . . ."), with police cars seemingly everywhere, their flashing blue and white lights coloring the bland cop faces, the curious guest faces, the surprised teenage faces. As some officers tossed the room for drugs, others checked IDs and collected names. The party was over.

But the fun wasn't. By the end of school Monday, news of the party had leaked back to coaches and administrators. Their initial reaction was very different than mine, which was simply to marvel at the audacity of high schoolers renting a motel room. The most my high school friends and I ever had the nerve to do was raid the liquor cabinet when our parents were out.

The athletic director asked the police across the river for the names of the students who'd attended the party, but, like a petulant kindergartner, they refused to share. So the district launched its own investigation.

Coaches and school administrators aren't exactly Sherlock Holmes. Their investigative methods, as Darla's friend's father described them, stopped just short of applying electrodes to tender body parts. First, every coach met with his or her team and passed around a sheet of paper, ordering anyone who'd attended the party to sign it. Those who were honest (or stupid) enough to put their names down were then hauled into the athletic director's office, where they were pressured to squeal on whoever else was there. The district, in others words, turned as if instinctively to some of the cruelest, most infamous practices of authoritarian regimes—self-denunciation and snitching.

Although the athletic director ended up with a long list of names, no one was actually kicked off a team, the prescribed punishment for breaking the pledge. To suspend so many players would have meant having to cancel the rest of the sports season. That, like requiring summer reading or allowing students to go to the bathroom without a pass, was a step the district wasn't prepared to take.

And neither were parents. In fact, many of them criticized the district for prying into their kids' off-campus activities. One mother even told the superintendent that she'd driven her soccer-player son to the motel. "At least that way I knew where he was," she said.

The assistant football coach frowned while relating all this. I can understand why. The episode raises a number of complex moral issues. Should school force students to make promises they might not be able to keep? When, if ever, is it right to snitch? Do sports build character? Or are school sports mostly a sham and primarily teach kids how to be rats and cheats and hypocrites?

THE ORCHARD OF BROKEN PROMISES

The Bible, which some would consider a pretty good source for moral guidance, divides promises into two categories. *Neder*, generally translated as "vow," refers to a promise to do something ("I vow to exercise more"), while *shevu'ah*, generally translated as "oath," implies a promise to abstain from doing something ("I swear to stop visiting Internet porn sites").[1] In either case, the Bible takes promises seriously. As Numbers 30:2 says, "When a man vows a vow to the Lord, or swears an oath to bind himself by a pledge, he shall not break his word; he shall do according to all that proceeds out of his mouth."

Because of the strict nature of promises, the later biblical books as well as rabbinic literature discourage people from making them. "It is better that you should not vow," Ecclesiastes 5:4 advises, "than that you should vow and fail." In the Talmud, Rabbi Judah states, "Better is he who vows and pays," but Rabbi Meir counters, "Better is he who does not vow at all." To break a promise is bad stuff, a sacrilege, and one way to keep your word, Jewish tradition suggests, is to not give it.[2]

But students must sign the pledge if they want to play high school sports. This puts them in a jam. By requiring the student athletes to forswear the use of tobacco, alcohol, or drugs, the district is essentially requiring them to lie. It just isn't realistic to expect your typical American teenager, subject to fierce peer pressure and eager for new experiences, not to try forbidden substances at least once or twice. Don't the adults in school remember what they did when they were young, or were they too wasted at the time for it to leave much of an impression?

Although district policy doesn't accommodate the reality of teenage life, local culture, interestingly, does. For years, high school kids have been holding parties in the abandoned orchards scattered throughout the community like the overgrown ruins of an earlier civilization. They drive their parents' cars and trucks back among the gnarled stunted trees, where they build a bonfire from old fruit crates and broken branches, then try to act cool by lighting up cigarettes and sucking down beers. The town cops always seem to know when there's an orchard party, materializing out of the darkness just before midnight, not to harass or arrest anyone but to dump the last of the beer on the ground, sort the drunks from the designated drivers, and send everyone home safe.

There's an unofficial agreement between the cops and the kids. The cops agree to let the kids be kids, and the kids agree not to get violently drunk and destroy a motel room. Understand, I'm not condoning underage drinking. I'm simply pointing out that forcing student athletes to make false promises can breed a certain cynicism toward promise keeping, which, in the long run, may harm them (and society) more than experimenting with alcohol, tobacco, or even drugs.

And it isn't only the Bible that tells us so. Philosophers also consider false promises dangerous. Immanuel Kant (1724–1804), who placed honesty and trust at the heart of his moral philosophy, believed that people have inherent value and that therefore they should be treated with respect—"always as an end and never as a means only." He envisioned the ideal moral community as "a kingdom of ends" in which no one is ever used or manipulated by anyone else and all act in ways they'd want others to act.[3]

Under Kant's formula, called the categorical imperative, it's wrong—categorically wrong—to make false promises.[4] When a person makes a false promise, he or she acts on a principle that can't be adopted by everyone, at least not and still have a good society. Falsely promising something undermines trust, and without trust, social relationships collapse, cooperation breaks down, and respect for other people disintegrates. Selfishness and suspicion become the order of the day, and the only attitude that seems worth cultivating is a kind of clever dishonesty.

For this reason, modern philosophers continue to attach enormous importance to promise keeping. Sissela Bok, for example, asked, "What is it . . . about promises . . . that endows them with such power?" and answered, "In the first place, in making a promise, I set up expectations, an equilibrium; should I break my promise, I upset the equilibrium and fail to live up to those expectations. Second, in breaking faith, I am failing to make my promise *come true*. If I make a promise, knowing I shall break it, I am lying."[5] And lies burn a hole in the world. Just look at the horrible damage done—the bombed-out cities, the oil-stained oceans, the laid-off workers—by the creamy lies of presidents and corporations.

Deep down, the district must know that most of the student athletes won't keep the pledge of no smoking, drinking, or drug use, and the student athletes must know it, too. By the one making a false promise and the other accepting it, both degrade the power of promises in general. The Bible may consider promises sacred and binding, but more and more people seem to consider them merely provisional—a temporary hang-up, a minor condition. Under these circumstances, it'd be better to have no pledge at all than a pledge that teaches it's okay to give your word and not really mean it.

SEASON OF THE WITCH

As if extracting a lying promise from student athletes weren't enough, the district also tried to lure them into being snitches. In doing so, it joined a growing trend. Snitching has practically become a required subject at many schools. Last spring, administrators at Glenbard North High School near Chicago offered $150 (that's a lot of video game rentals from Blockbuster) for information on the identities of students involved in a food fight.[6]

It wasn't always so. There was a time when snitching was seen as the lowest form of human behavior. Even career criminals looked down on it. They ranked informers somewhere below sex offenders in the prison hierarchy.[7]

Language still reflects the disrepute in which informers were once held. The *Cassell Dictionary of Slang* lists about 200 words, dating back to the seventeenth century, used to describe an informer, and most of them—from "bleater" to "fink" to "weasel" to "rat"—brim with contempt.[8]

Nor does the Bible seem to approve of snitching. Genesis 37:2 suggests that the tragic conflict between Joseph and his brothers started when he snitched to his father about their misconduct.[9] Then there's the "world's best known snitch," Judas Iscariot.[10] Judas's betrayal of Jesus to the Romans for thirty pieces of silver was so vile that 2,000 years later his very name is a common insult.

Snitches also figured in a couple of the darkest, most disturbing episodes in American history. A group of young girls sparked the infamous Salem Witch Trials of 1692 by claiming, under pressure from Puritan leaders, that some old widows had bewitched them. As panic gripped the village, the number of accusers and accusations multiplied. Ultimately, fourteen women and six men were tried, convicted, and executed, all on the basis of false stories and forced confessions.[11]

During the 1950s, there was another kind of witch hunt. Senator Joseph McCarthy of Wisconsin, whose name has since become synonymous with demagoguery, chaired sensational public hearings into communist infiltration of the U.S. government. Many witnesses saved their own skins by ratting on close colleagues.[12]

Popular culture has had very little positive to say about such behavior. In George Orwell's disutopian novel *1984*, spies and snitches shore up a totalitarian regime, while in John Ford's Oscar-winning movie *The Informer*, Victor McLaglen plays a pathetic creature who sells out an Irish Republican Army compatriot to the Black and Tans. McLaglen's character, Gypo Nolan, discovers to his bewilderment that no one will shield a squealer. Broken, drunk, and shunned, he's shot down on a dark Dublin street for his treachery.

But if Hollywood loathes a rat, it loves a whistleblower. Apparently, snitching is morally justified when done from selfless motives and for honest ends—the case with Marlon Brando's character in *On the Waterfront*. Director Elia Kazan intended the 1954 movie as a defense of his own testimony before the House Un-American Activities Committee. There's quite a difference, though, between snitching on a corrupt union boss, as Brando does, and delivering powerless friends and associates into the hands of blacklisting McCarthyites, as Kazan did.[13]

The distinction is utterly lost on those trying to enforce student discipline back at my local high school. When the coaches and administrators pressured the student athletes to snitch on friends, they seem to have had no idea that they were encouraging questionable moral behavior. How do people get so obtuse? More to the point, how do such people get into positions of influence and authority over kids? And what can we do to correct it? Reason with them? Plead with them? Hit them in the head with a nunchak?

To be fair, many other districts have resorted to the use of student snitches and in a much bigger way. The school board in

Portsmouth, New Hampshire, recently approved a program to pay high schoolers up to $100 for crime tips, prompting the local paper to run a cartoon with a valedictorian, salutatorian, and "snitch-atorian." In Charlotte, North Carolina, a similar program has expanded from the high schools down to the middle schools. It's promoted on fifty-three campuses with posters and stickers bearing an Orwellian logo—a pair of eyes under the paranoia-inducing warning "Who's Watching?" followed by a hotline number. Elsewhere around the country, districts tempt students to snitch on classmates with prizes of T-shirts, gift certificates, pizzas, and autographed baseballs.[14]

More than one researcher has remarked on the similarity of these programs to *America's Most Wanted*, a TV show that asks viewers to hurry to the phone and report anyone who resembles the actors staging the "hokey crime re-creations" on the screen.[15] But whether inspired by TV or, as also seems likely, the Columbine shootings and the events of 9/11, school snitch programs give off an ominous vibe.

Whatever happened to tolerance, openness, and trust? Whatever happened to teaching and practicing the values of a free society? When did school become Stalinist Russia?

Many criminologists find the notion of bribing students to turn snitch theoretically unsound and morally repugnant. "The kind of school environment that is conducive to positive school behavior," Denise Gottfredson, a leading expert on school-based crime prevention, said, "is one in which students feel they belong and trust one another." Dennis Rosenbaum, head of the Criminal Justice Department at the University of Illinois–Chicago, agreed. Student snitches "may have some beneficial effect," he conceded, "but is it worth creating the fear and mistrust and other possible negative effects that you introduce . . . ? If we continue in that direction, then we will have a society that consists of gates and cameras and anonymous reporting."[16]

As the quintessential democratic institution, free and open to all, the American public school has a responsibility to encourage students to behave like freedom-loving citizens, not like KGB informants. Novelist E. M. Forster once said, "If I had to choose between betraying my country and betraying my friend, I hope I should I have the guts to betray my country."[17] Most of us probably don't share Forster's extreme view, though we might if we lived in a country that was rounding up Jews for extermination or that sponsored international terrorism. Loyalty is a virtue only when exercised in the service of a virtuous cause.

The student athletes who were interrogated in the athletic director's office about the motel party had to decide to what or whom they should be loyal. Truth? Authority? Friends? There was no automatic answer, but the coaches and administrators expected, even demanded, one. Just about the worst thing schools can do is accustom students to thinking that the answers to knotty moral questions are obvious. Students, whether they decide to snitch or not, should at least struggle with the decision, feel "a sense of moral burden."[18] By weighing the painful alternatives— tell a lie or hurt a friend?—they start to appreciate the moral complexity of everyday life.

It is, in fact, so morally complex that some people need special help to navigate it. A number of them turn to Randy Cohen, "The Ethicist" from the *New York Times Magazine*. The question he most often receives is "Do I tell?"—"about the infidelity of a friend's spouse, the kickbacks extorted by a co-worker, the shoplifting of a granny in a grocery store," and so on.[19] A former writer for *Late Night with David Letterman*, his responses have, for all their loopy humor, a surprising depth, like a pierced and tattooed teenager with an unexpected aptitude for Hegelian dialectics.

Although Cohen has never directly addressed a situation like that of the student athletes, he has written about honor codes. He has no real issue with codes that forbid students to lie, cheat, or steal but balks at those that also require them to snitch on peers who do. One part of his objection is that the latter provision is nearly always impossible to enforce. As he observes, there's a long-standing taboo in kid culture against ratting out another kid. The other part of his objection stems from a general skepticism about snitching. Why try to run others people's lives when we have enough trouble already trying to run our own? "The happiest outcome," he concludes, "would be for your school to abolish such dubious codes."[20]

For my district to order student athletes to make a promise they aren't likely to keep may be pretty stupid, but to order them to snitch on each other for breaking the promise is even stupider. It isn't as if some great wrong—the torture of political prisoners, for example, or a plot to plunder employee pension funds—would've gone undiscovered if the students didn't talk. The most that would've happened is that school authorities would've had a few less names on their hit list.

There should be a stigma attached to being a squealer, a stoolie, a snitch. A society in which people rat to the authorities for pay or self-protection is the stuff of Orwellian nightmares. But this isn't science fiction, and we aren't dreaming. School is a paranoid fantasy suddenly come to life, a murky place of shifting moral boundaries where some other kid can tell on you and win (yea!) a coupon for free pizza.

"WAR MINUS THE SHOOTING"

Darla was just about to reach the safety of the chorus room when the vice principal, a squat, dyspeptic woman, busted her for wearing a halter top in violation of the student dress code.

"Come with me," the vice principal said and led the way down the hall. Once inside her closetlike office, she scowled at Darla for what seemed a long time. When she finally spoke, it was to ask in a sharp voice, "Do you play a sport?"

The question secretly struck Darla, who runs as if she were born without full control over her limbs, as hilarious. But when she told me about it after school that day, I wasn't amused. Behind the question lay the widespread belief, more than a century old, that sports build character.

Sports are supposed to teach self-sacrifice, discipline, fair play, and respect for authority. Through sports, kids are supposed to learn to get their kicks on the field or in the gym and not with drugs and alcohol.[21] If Darla played a sport, the vice principal reasoned, then she was part of the moral elite of the school, someone the rest of the kids can look up to, and wearing the halter top was probably just an innocent mistake. But if she didn't play a sport, who knew what kind of evil freak she was and what other awful deeds she might be contemplating?

There's only one thing wrong with this picture of sports as the salvation of American youth—it isn't true.

Andrew W. Miracle Jr. and C. Roger Rees, who examined forty years of research on tens of thousands of athletes at all levels of competition, found "little empirical evidence that sport builds character or has any positive effects on youth." If anything, most of the research suggested that participation in sports increases "moral callousness."[22] A Canadian study reported, for example, that the longer boys played on youth hockey teams, the more likely they were to accept cheating and violence and to use illegal tactics.[23] Perhaps Orwell wasn't exaggerating when he said, "Serious sport has nothing to do with fair play. It is bound up with hatred, jealousy, boastfulness, disregard of all rules and sadistic pleasure in witnessing violence. In other words, it is war minus the shooting."[24]

Need more proof that playing a sport might not be the character-building activity many claim it is? Then turn your TV to ESPN or glance through the sports section of the newspaper. What do you find? Colorado Rockies pitcher Denny Neagle, married and with two small children, caught driving around Denver with a prostitute. Swim star Michael Phelps, six-time gold medal winner at the 2004 Olympics, arrested for drunk driving. Ron Artest, Stephen Jackson, Anthony Johnson, David Harrison, and Jermaine O'Neal, players for the Indiana Pacers, charged with assault and battery after storming into the bleachers in Detroit and beating up fans.[25]

Moral callousness isn't limited to athletes at the highest levels either. "You think that doesn't trickle down?" Bruce Brown, author of *Teaching Character Through Sport*, said. He blamed youth league and school coaches who get their concept of what it takes to reach the top from ESPN, then drum it into kids' heads.[26]

A recent survey of 4,200 high school athletes, conducted by the Josephson Institute of Ethics, tends to bear him out. Although 90 percent of the athletes said their coaches set a good example of fair play and sportsmanship, it wasn't clear they knew what a good example was. Large percentages endorsed questionable actions by coaches, from arguing with an official in order to influence future calls to instructing players how to illegally hold and push opponents without getting caught to using a stolen playbook of another team.[27]

The survey revealed that the athletes, particularly males, had difficulty distinguishing morally sound strategy from win-at-all-costs trickery. Fifty-eight percent of the males thought it proper to deliberately inflict pain in football to intimidate an opponent; 47 percent, to trash-talk a defender after every score ("Put on some makeup, pretty boy!"); 30 percent, to throw at a batter who homered last time up; 27 percent, to soak a football field to slow down an opponent; and 25 percent, to illegally alter a hockey stick.[28]

Perhaps most troubling, the athletes were inclined to apply "game reasoning"—that is, if you aren't caught bending the rules, nothing wrong happened—to nonsports situations.[29] Fifty-six percent of males and 45 percent of females agreed with the statement, "In the real world, successful people do what they have to do to win even if others consider it cheating," while 43 percent of males and 27 percent of females agreed with the statement, "A person has to lie or cheat sometimes in order to succeed." The "person" might as well have been the athletes themselves. Sixty-eight percent of both males and females admitted to cheating on a test in school in the past year.[30]

The Duke of Wellington famously declared that the Battle of Waterloo was won on the playing fields of Eton. Commenting on the survey results, Michael Josephson, the institute's president, said, "It appears that today's playing fields are the breeding grounds for the next generation of corporate pirates and political scoundrels." Josephson assumed, just like the Iron Duke, that sports build character but was far less optimistic about the kind of character under construction. He saw the survey as showing that a malignant, do-whatever-you-gotta-do-to-win coaching philosophy had crept into high school sports and left the athletes confused, "floating in moral relativism and self-serving rationalizations."[31]

Despite all the evidence to the contrary—doping scandals, research findings, O. J.—most people still believe that sports have a positive effect on character (and, in addition, on their kids' chances for a college scholarship). As Jay Coakley, a sports sociologist at the University of Colorado–Colorado Springs, noted, "There are just so many things vested in those beliefs. People have used them in decisions on how to raise their kids, have spent hours, years watching sports, have funded them through their tax monies. It's really hard to abandon this line of thinking."[32] Countless communities around the country treat high school sports as sacred, an American institution somewhere between Thanksgiving and going to the mall. To criticize sports or to suggest that school taxes might perhaps be better spent on textbooks and teachers can cause people to look at you in alarm, as if they'd caught you boiling the family dog for dinner.

The sacredness of high school sports practically guarantees worship of the "jocks" who play them. Is anyone the least bit surprised that research has found that male athletes are at the top of the status hierarchy in most high schools?[33] Just watch a few teen movies. No matter how exaggerated they seem in other regards, the movies are remarkably accurate when it comes to portraying the power relations among school cliques. The jocks, effortlessly handsome and surrounded by a gaggle of sexy cheerleader girlfriends, are always shown reigning over the "brains," the "band fags," and the "burnouts" with the casual sadism of medieval lords.

But though this kind of behavior may be entertaining in movies, it can be disastrous in real life.

In August 2003, at a football camp in Pennsylvania, three varsity players on Long Island's Mempham High School football team sexually assaulted three junior varsity players at night and in between practices as part of an initiation. (A grand jury later said the five coaches who chaperoned the trip were "more concerned with being coaches of a football team than interested in the well-being of the players.") Often as many as a dozen teammates watched and cheered while the victims were held down and sodomized with pinecones, golf balls, and a broomstick. ("The coaches displayed a lack of common-sense accountability when it came to managing or running the camp," the grand jury reported. "It is unfortunately abundantly clear that the coaches did not know that the crimes committed by their players were being perpetrated.") Duct tape and loud rock music muffled the victims' screams.[34]

After the attacks became public knowledge, some criticized the school for allowing the chief culprit, a junior named Ken Carney, to attend the camp despite a long disciplinary record. Carney once cursed out the umpire at a baseball game, then shouted and swore at his coach. Another time he made a sexual threat in class against a female teacher. It seemed to his teammates that Carney could get away with anything.[35]

"We build athletes up as the symbolic protectors of school and community pride," Miracle and Rees observed, "treat them like demigods, sometimes place them above the laws of the school and community, and then shake our heads in confusion and disbelief when they occasionally call our bluff."[36] The mixed local reaction to the Mempham scandal was a case in point. At school, other students teased the victims, calling them "broomstick boy" and "butt pirate." Three people who spoke out against the coaching staff received death threats in the mail. And though the Bellmore-Merrick Central High School District canceled the Mempham football season and fired the coaches, residents grumbled about it.[37]

Compared to the nightmarish events at the football camp, the party at the motel may seem almost trivial. But, in fact, both were rooted in the same cultural contradiction. On the one hand, student athletes are expected to be, as my district's policy puts it, "school representatives" who display "appropriate behavior" on and off the field.[38] On the other, many of them feel compelled to live up to the "macho image" of the beer-guzzling, sex-crazed jock.[39] The two elements exist in eternal conflict, like God and the Devil or Clearsil and zits.

The sexual and drinking exploits of student athletes are the very lifeblood of school gossip. Nonetheless, some of those who attended the motel party were never caught, and the ones who were caught were never punished. Not a single player was thrown off a team or given detention or even sent for counseling. The athletic director blamed a lack of hard evidence; more likely, he was simply afraid of the insane uproar that canceling fall sports would've caused. He'd launched his investigation, which stretched over several days and involved dozens of interviews, as a show of concern, a sign that the district wouldn't tolerate student drinking and drug use. But all it actually showed, when it got down to the end, was the district's hypocrisy.

Allowing the sports season to go on had the effect of reinforcing the split between the straight, conformist behavior of the athletes in public—for example, wearing a tie to school on game day—and their drunkenness and promiscuity in private. Even worse, it may have given them the feeling that they were somehow bulletproof, immune from the usual penalties and repercussions of rule breaking. At its extreme, this sense of invulnerability can lead to serious crimes—such as shoving a golf ball dipped in Mineral Ice, an external ointment used for sore muscles, up a fourteen-year-old boy's ass.

You may have concluded from everything I've written so far that I hate sports. I don't. In high school, I ran cross-country and track, and later, as a parent of four growing kids, I coached Little League and youth soccer. Baseball has always been my favorite sport to play or watch, and I especially enjoyed teaching nine- and ten-year-olds who'd just gotten their first mitts how to go back on a fly ball and stay down on a grounder.

But sports per se don't build character. As Joel Fisher, author of *101 Ways to Be a Terrific Sports Parent*, said, "It's not automatic that if you throw a uniform on a kid, he'll learn life skills."[40] He may learn the exact opposite—cheating, lying, and bad sportsmanship. No one who has studied the issue seems to doubt that sports have the potential to facilitate moral development. For sports to actually do it, though, would require "a vastly different coach methodology and participation environment."[41] That is, coaches would have to make character building rather than winning their number one priority.

The pledge that the student athletes in my district must sign has a preamble full of lofty assurances about the positive nature of high school sports. It claims that the sports program is "an extension and integral part of the total educational curriculum." It calls on "all concerned with athletics," from coaches to parents to fans, to "recognize that the purpose of athletics is to promote the physical, mental, moral, social, and emotional well being of the individual players." It states, "Sportsmanship reveals character and should be emphasized at all times."[42] But saying these things isn't the same as doing them, and saying them without doing them sets the wrong example for kids.

Those athletes who went to the party at the motel let down their coaches and school. They shouldn't have been there, and they sure as hell shouldn't have been drinking. But, by the same token, the adults in charge of the school and its sports program let down the athletes. Whatever lesson the adults intended to teach—and I assume it wasn't something morally toxic—what they did teach was promise breaking, snitching, and smug indifference to threats of punishment. If the whole episode had been a game, it would have been an oddly joyless one, unfolding before a chilled crowd and according to no discernible rules, and the score would have been nothing to nothing when play, already many hours long, was halted on account of darkness.

NOTES

1. Jordan D. Cohen, "Holy Words," My Jewish Learning.com, http://www.myjewishlearning.com/texts/Weekly_Torah_Commentary/mattot_kolel5762_... (accessed November 11, 2004).

2. Cohen, "Holy Words."

3. Alison Hills, "Kantian Trust," The Open University, www.open2.net/trust/society/soc_kant/soc_kant2.htm (accessed December 1, 2004).

4. For an excellent summary of Kantian ethics, see Roger J. Sullivan, *An Introduction to Kant's Ethics* (Cambridge: Cambridge University Press, 1994).

5. Sissela Bok, *Lying: Moral Choice in Public and Private Life* (New York: Pantheon, 1978), 152.

6. Jack Komperda, "School Seeking Food Fight Snitches," *Chicago Daily Herald* (Chicago suburbs), May 29, 2004, 1.

7. Duncan Campell, "A Nation of Snouts, Finks and Snitches," *Guardian*, October 12, 2004, n.p.

8. Campell, "A Nation of Snouts, Finks and Snitches."

9. Asher Meir, "The Jewish Ethicist: Snitching," asih.com, http://www.aish.com/SSI/societyWork/work/The_Jewish_... (accessed November 19, 2004).

10. Jim Redden, *Snitch Culture* (Venice, Calif.: Feral Press, 2000), 7.

11. Redden, *Snitch Culture*, 54.

12. Redden, *Snitch Culture*, 8.

13. Michael Sandel and Christopher Buckley, "When Is It OK to Betray a Friend?" *Slate*, http://slate.msn.com/id/21255 (accessed November 19, 2004).

14. Mark Fritz, "Learning Fascism in American Schools," http://www.worldfreeinternet.net/news/mwsl120.htm (accessed November 19, 2004). This is a reprint of an article published in the *Los Angeles Times*, Orange County edition, May 3, 1998.

15. Fritz, "Learning Fascism in American Schools"; Redden, *Snitch Culture*, 3.

16. Fritz, "Learning Fascism in American Schools."

17. Quoted in Sandel and Buckley, "When Is It OK to Betray a Friend?"

18. Sandel and Buckley, "When Is It OK to Betray a Friend?"

19. Randy Cohen, *The Good, the Bad and the Difference* (New York: Broadway Books, 2002), 6.

20. Cohen, *The Good, the Bad and the Difference*, 227.

21. Andrew W. Miracle Jr. and C. Roger Rees, *Lessons of the Locker Room: The Myth of School Sports* (Amherst, N.Y.: Prometheus Books, 1994), 17. There used to be a bumper sticker that read, "Kids in Sports Stay Out of Courts."

22. Miracle and Rees, *Lessons of the Locker Room*, 8.

23. "Knocks for Jocks—Benefits of High School Sports Debunked," *Psychology Today*, http://wwww.findarticles.com/p/articles/mi_m1165/is_n6_v27/ai_15868226 (accessed November 22, 2004).

24. I found this quotation at Thinkexist.com, http://em.thinkexist
.com/common (accessed December 2, 2004).

25. Greg Couch, "Character Study: Money a Bad Influence on Sports,"
Chicago Sun-Times, http://www.suntimes.com/cgi-bin (accessed November 23, 2004).

26. Quoted in Couch, "Character Study."

27. "New Survey Shows High School Sports Filled with Cheating, Improper Gamesmanship and Confusion about Sportsmanship," Sportsmanship Survey 2004, http://charactercounts.org/sports/survey2004/ (accessed November 22, 2004).

28. "New Survey."

29. Miracle and Rees, *Lessons of the Locker Room*, 92.

30. "New Survey."

31. "New Survey."

32. Quoted in Couch, "Character Study."

33. Miracle and Rees, *Lessons of the Locker Room*, 67.

34. Karla Schuster and Keiko Morris, "Appalled and Sickened,"
Newsday.com, http://www.newsday.com/sports/highschool/ny-limeph
11370324,mar11,0,5936367 (accessed December 1, 2004).

35. Brian Harmon, "Ringleader of Hazing Pack," *New York Daily News*,
December 20, 2003, n.p.

36. Miracle and Rees, *Lessons of the Locker Room*, 121.

37. Harmon, "Ringleader of Hazing Pack."

38. "Sports Participation Policy," Highland (N.Y.) Central School District, November 9, 2004, unpaged photocopy.

39. Miracle and Rees, *Lessons of the Locker Room*, 73–74.

40. Quoted in Couch, "Character Study."

41. Sharon K. Stoll and Jennifer M. Beller, "Do Sports Build Character?" in *Sports in School: The Future of an Institution*, ed. John R. Gerdy
(New York: Teachers College Press, 2000), 27.

42. "Sports Participation Policy," unpaged.

3

TWILIGHT'S LAST GLEAMING

It'd been a beautiful spring day. Then Darla brought home from school her ninth-grade schedule for me to sign, and the day wasn't so beautiful anymore.

The schedule listed every course available to next year's ninth graders, with a check beside the ones Darla would be taking— Math A, Earth Science, English, Spanish II, Physical Education, Studio Art, and Chorus. It was a moment before I realized that a social studies course wasn't there. I have three older children who went through the high school, and they all took social studies in ninth grade. But now, for some reason, social studies was gone.

Social studies is Darla's favorite subject. She even talks about being a social studies teacher when she grows up—that is, if she doesn't make it as an FBI agent/supermodel.

I pointed out the absence of social studies to Darla.

"Yeah, I know," she said. "The guidance counselor explained it."

I wondered how anyone in the post–9/11 world could possibly explain not teaching social studies to fourteen-year-olds. It isn't as if kids graduate from high school well informed about history or politics or current events. In 2000, only 5 percent of Americans ages eighteen to twenty-five reported that they followed public affairs.[1]

The ancient Greeks had a name for people who took no interest in the life of the *polis*. They were called "idiots."[2]

My wife, Barbara, who's calmer and more charitable than I, phoned the high school principal to find out what had happened to ninth-grade social studies. He told her that there was no state law requiring it be offered. Besides, he said, other districts in the county had dropped it years ago. Our district was finally catching up.

As Barbara recounted the conversation to me at dinner, I sat in stunned silence. I'd always thought the idea was to emulate the best practices of other districts. When had it become to emulate the worst?

> *A popular government without popular information, or the means of acquiring it, is but a Prologue to a Farce or a Tragedy; or perhaps both. And the people who mean to be their own Governors must arm themselves with the power knowledge gives.*
>
> —James Madison

Until the 1960s, high school students took as many as three courses in civics, democracy, and American government. Today, most students graduate from high school having taken only one course in government, usually in twelfth grade, which may be "too little and too late" to leave much of an impression. According to a 2004 survey, 30 percent of Americans said they'd never had a course in civics or government or couldn't remember if they had.[3]

Social studies education for elementary school students has also diminished. Between 1988 and 1998, the proportion of fourth graders receiving a daily lesson in social studies fell from 49 to 39 percent. It should perhaps come as no surprise, then, that in 1998 one-third of fourth graders couldn't identify the meaning of "I pledge allegiance to the flag" on the National Assessment of Educational Progress (NAEP) in civics.[4]

Older students fared no better on the exam, popularly known as the "Nation's Report Card." About one-third of eighth and twelfth graders couldn't demonstrate a basic understanding of how American government works. And twelfth graders did even worse on the NAEP in U.S. history in 2001, with 57 percent scoring below basic, "an achievement level that denotes only partial mastery of significant historical knowledge and analytical skills." Asked to pick a U.S. ally in World War II from a list of countries, more than half thought the answer was Italy, Germany, or Japan.[5]

As much as a lack of social studies courses contributed to these dismal results, so has a lack of knowledgeable teachers in the courses offered. A high school government teacher recently attended a summer institute on the history of American political thought conducted by the Center for Civic Education. When the teacher completed the program, he said he wished he could bring back all the students he'd taught over the past thirteen years. He would correct the misconceptions he'd given them.[6]

This was hardly the first or last teacher to give students wrong information. Several years ago, the center studied how well high school government teachers could explain fifty-five key concepts in their field, including popular sovereignty, checks and balances, federalism, and judicial review. More than 50 percent couldn't explain many of the concepts well at all.[7]

There's something almost criminal about putting kids in classes with teachers who aren't knowledgeable in the subjects they purport to teach. As educator and writer Deborah Meier pointed out, "We wouldn't send a child to a soccer camp run by people who don't know how to play soccer."[8] Yet more than half of all students in history and world civilization classes are being taught by teachers who neither majored nor minored in history. And the percentage of students in civics and government classes being taught by teachers without majors or minors in political science is even greater.[9]

No nation has ever had the luxury of turning out citizens who don't possess a modicum of civic competence. Charles N. Quigley, executive director of the Center for Civic Education, has estimated that, at most, 15 percent of precollege students receive an adequate education in civics.[10] This means that the vast majority of students are "idiots" in the ancient Greek sense of the word—unschooled in democratic principles and unaccustomed to democratic participation. It also means, of course, that the future of American democracy is in very shaky hands.

> *Those who prize liberty only instrumentally for the externals it brings—ease, comfort, riches—are not destined to keep it long.*
>
> —Alexis de Tocqueville

Representative Roger Wicker was visiting the Advanced Placement history class at a high school in his Mississippi congressional district. When he asked the students, all seniors, to name some of the unalienable rights listed in the Declaration of Independence, he got silence. Apparently, these truths weren't so self-evident.

Wicker gave the students a hint. "Among these are life," he said, "and . . ."

"Death?" one student ventured.[11]

> *Preach a crusade against ignorance. . . . Establish and improve the law for educating the common people. . . . General education will enable every man to judge for himself what will secure or endanger his freedom.*
>
> —Thomas Jefferson

Forty state constitutions mention the importance of civic literacy for citizens, and thirteen of them say the central purpose of public schools is to promote good citizenship, democracy, and free government. Moreover, curriculum guidelines in every state note the need for civics education, even if the subject seldom gets the kind of attention in grades K through 12 it deserves.[12]

From the very beginning of the republic, the more farsighted saw that democratic participation is "a learned behavior that must be taught and taught well."[13] In 1778, as a member of the Virginia Assembly, Jefferson drafted "A Bill for the More General Diffusion of Knowledge," which would've guaranteed three years of public schooling for all children, with scholarships to secondary school and university for a select few. The bill came up for a vote three times between 1779 and 1817, and each time was defeated. "There is a snail-paced gait for the advance of new ideas," a frustrated Jefferson groused. "People have more feeling for canals and roads than for education."[14]

Although Jefferson's dream of statewide school systems began to be realized in the 1830s, it wasn't until the turn of the twentieth century that a specific curriculum for civics education emerged. Between 1890 and 1930, more than 22 million immigrants, including almost 3 million children, arrived in the United States. Schools became the focal point of the effort to "Americanize" the "huddled masses yearning to breathe free." Ellwood Cubberley, one of the leading educators of the era, explained that the goal of Americanization was "to assimilate and amalgamate these people as part of our American race, to implant in their children, so far as can be done, the Anglo-Saxon conception of righteousness, law and order, and popular government, and to awaken in them a reverence for our democratic institutions and for those things in our national life which we as a people hold to be of abiding worth."[15]

Americanization involved offering at school, among other courses, several in civics and American history. These tended to be "catechistic and dull" and stressed the nation's triumphs while ignoring its failings. Nonetheless, this kind of instruction continued for more than half a century, sustained by the patriotic fervor of two world wars and the paranoia of the early years of the Cold War.[16]

Then came the turmoil of the 1960s and 1970s. The sanitized version of American history and politics that had long been taught to students was challenged by the ugly realities of the Vietnam War and Watergate. In addition, the civil rights movement caused a surge in ethnic and racial pride that made the idea of a core culture to which all groups should subscribe seem oppressive. Everywhere were signs of disillusionment, rebellion, a crumbling consensus about what the United States represented. As a result, many schools dropped requirements for civics education.[17]

Today, even the strongest advocates of civics education aren't in favor of reviving the traditional civics class, which was never noted for portraying the American political system as it was or for stimulating student interest. They recognize that a return to the days of teachers who emphasized rote memorization of facts and textbooks that contained dry accounts of procedures (how a bill becomes law and so on) is unlikely to benefit students. It may actually further alienate them from politics.[18]

But if a class or two in civics isn't enough to reverse young people's ignorance and apathy, what is? A growing body of research suggests that in order to turn things around, civics education must become central to schooling, a major item on the agenda of every course in every classroom. Or, as political scientist Amy Gutmann put it, "We can conclude that 'political education'—the cultivation of the virtues, knowledge, and skills necessary for political participation—has moral primacy over other purposes of public education in a democratic society."[19]

> *All who have meditated on the art of governing mankind have been convinced that the fate of empires depends on the education of youth.*
>
> —Aristotle

When my oldest daughter, Brittany, was a senior in high school, she made a film about the war in Iraq for class. The film was less than five minutes long but had the grip of a police choke hold.

It showed Brittany asking a number of her classmates, most of whom had just voiced support for the war, to locate Iraq on a blank world map. They couldn't. One after another pointed to the Iberian Peninsula or the Horn of Africa or Southeast Asia.

During the first Gulf War, comedian A. Whitney Brown had cracked, "Our bombs are smarter than the average high school student. At least they can find Kuwait." Brittany's film illustrated that very little had changed the second time around.

The film was accepted at a teen film festival. After it was screened, the audience had a chance to ask Brittany about it. A well-dressed man who might have been a Hollywood talent scout wondered how school officials could let such a damaging indictment of the educational system out of the district.

"Didn't any of your teachers see it?" he asked.

"Yeah," Brittany said.

"What did they say?"

Brittany shrugged. "Nothing."

> *Many public-school children seem to know only two dates—1492 and 4th of July; and as a rule they don't know what happened on either occasion.*
>
> —Mark Twain

If you have a morbid sense of humor or just don't give a crap about the fate of democracy, you can get a pretty good chuckle out of Americans' appalling lack of political knowledge and interest. Some examples:

- According to a recent survey, 80 percent of fifteen- to twenty-six-year-olds knew the hometown of the Simpson cartoon family, but less than 50 percent knew the political party of their state's governor, and only 40 percent could name the party that controls Congress.[20]

- Twenty-five percent of the fourth graders who took the NAEP U.S. history exam in 2001 didn't know that the Fourth of July celebrates the Declaration of Independence. They thought it marked the end of the Civil War, the arrival of the Pilgrims, or the start of women's right to vote.[21]
- More people watched the final episodes of *Cheers*, *M*A*S*H*, and *Seinfeld* than voted for the president of the United States in the 2000 election.[22]
- A study by the National Constitution Center found that only 38 percent of respondents could name all three branches of government. In a poll conducted two years earlier, 59 percent of all Americans could name the Three Stooges.[23]

Of course, not everyone thinks this is funny. Educators have begun to realize that American democracy is facing a crisis and that schools have a role to play in solving it. They can't seem to agree, though, on just what the role is. Is it teaching students to be honest and kind or historically minded and politically savvy? Is it developing students into good neighbors who respect each other's rights or citizen activists who protest injustice? The answer depends on whom you ask.

In 2004, pollsters for the Campaign for the Civic Mission of Schools asked 1,219 Americans over age eighteen to identify the qualities that make a good citizen. The qualities they named most often were providing for yourself and your family financially (86 percent), obeying the law (84 percent), and voting in elections (73 percent). The only other quality named by more than half the respondents was staying informed on news and major issues (55 percent).[24]

When added together, these responses amount to a vision of citizenship that's largely devoid of politics. Nor is there anything intrinsically democratic about it. People who work hard, pay their bills, and obey the law may be admirable, but they'd be just as welcome in a dictatorship as in a democracy.

The vision of the good citizen as someone who behaves in a personally responsible manner may owe its prevalence to the character education programs that many schools have adopted. The programs encourage traditional moral values, such as integrity, self-discipline, patriotism, and service. What the programs don't encourage—and may, in fact, discourage—is "the kind of critical reflection, dialogue, and action that are essential in a democratic society."[25] Participating in, say, a food drive is a nice thing for students to do but by itself won't get them to question why millions are hungry or teach them how to use the political process to fight the monster of hunger.

> *What good fortune for those in power that people do not think.*
>
> —Adolf Hitler

It's December 2002. The aircraft carrier USS *Abraham Lincoln* lurks in the Persian Gulf, poised for war. Darla and other middle school students are enlisted by their health teacher to send Christmas greetings to the sailors aboard.

The local newspaper interviews the teacher. She says the class project reinforces good citizenship, trustworthiness, caring, respect, honesty, responsibility, and fairness—the core values of Project Wisdom, the school's character education program. Although the story is meant to be uplifting, I read it over morning coffee with a sinking heart.

Why, I wonder, must good citizenship always be equated with militarism? Why can't students ever be encouraged to do something for peace? Isn't peace also worth teaching and, besides, more in keeping with the spirit of the season?

A couple months later, Barbara and I are sitting in the audience at a middle school concert. The chorus launches into a rousing rendition of Lee Greenwood's red-blooded, flag-waving "I'm Proud to Be an American." When the song ends, there is wild and prolonged applause. Everyone knows a lopsided war with Iraq is coming. The only question is how soon.

My head feels like a crumpled ball of paper. The evening has turned into a pep rally for God and country and war. And Darla is up there on stage, one of the cheerleaders!

I pour out my anger and frustration to Barbara as we are driving home. "Why do they have to sing that shit? It's a song for rednecks and crypto-fascists. Why can't they sing something that sticks it to authority?" I'm thinking of Pete Seeger's "Where Have All the Flowers Gone?" or Bob Dylan's "Blowin' in the Wind."

Barbara looks at me with pity. "Because people don't want to stick it to authority," she says.

> *I know of no safe depository of the ultimate powers of society but the people themselves, and if we think [the people] not enlightened enough to exercise their control with wholesome discretion the remedy is not to take it from them, but to inform their discretion by education.*
>
> —Thomas Jefferson

In the wake of 9/11, civics education has increasingly assumed an antidemocratic cast. Nebraska's state legislature, for example, introduced Bill 982, which would require each school board to appoint a committee on "Americanism" to see that schools arrange "curriculum in such a way that the love of . . . America will be instilled in the hearts and minds of the youth of the state." The bill was defeated, but the Nebraska State Board of Education jumped in, directing that the high school social studies curriculum should emphasize "the benefits and advantages of our government," that the middle school social studies curriculum should "instill a love of country," and that the elementary school social studies curriculum should include the "exploits and deeds of American heroes, singing patriotic songs, memorizing 'The Star Spangled Banner' and 'America,' and reverence for the flag."[26]

The leading experts on civics education are distressed by the attempts to foster a gung-ho, John Wayne, "my country right or wrong" kind of patriotism. It would be one thing if we lived in a military state, such as ancient Sparta, but we don't—not yet. When the experts outline the skills and attitudes that patriotic citizens in a democracy need, obedience to authority isn't high on the list.

What is? "Thoughtful habits," in Deborah Meier's phrase. Roger Soder identifies these as "patience, tolerance for ambiguity, and an aversion to either/or 'solutions,'" while Melissa K. Comber sums them up as "the ability to critically think about civic and political life." Similarly, Richard Pratte observes, "A thinking loyalty, rather than an unthinking loyalty, is fundamental to a just democratic society."[27]

Also high on the list are what Pratte calls "social-action skills." Joseph Kahane and Joel Westheimer define these as "the skills people need to exert power over issues that affect their lives." To Pratte, social-action skills suggest "the ability to confer, discuss, debate, argue, plan, negotiate, compromise, and so forth." To Kahane and Westheimer, they include "how to work in a group, speak in public, forge coalitions among varied interests, and protest or petition for change." Nel Noddings says such skills, along with concern for the rights and welfare of others, are indispensable for "'get[ting] about' in an environment of political freedom."[28]

Most of the experts would add something else to the list—an awareness of the tension between liberty and order. If the responsibilities of democratic citizenship can't be met by simply displaying the flag or slapping a "Support Our Troops" magnet on the rear of a car, neither can they be met by "an overly zealous and critical attitude" toward the government. Pratte, Soder, and others stress the need to maintain perspective, to keep negativism as well as patriotism "within the bounds of reason and prudence."[29]

So we do have some idea of what good citizens in a democracy—as distinct from good people in any kind of society—should be like. They should be informed and thoughtful. They should be tolerant of others. They should be ready to work together to overcome problems. They should be skeptical of demagoguery. They should be able to strike a reasonable balance between rights and responsibilities.

We even have some idea of how to teach these things. The 2003 Carnegie Corporation report *The Civic Mission of Schools* cites at least five methods that researchers consider promising:[30]

- Increase formal instruction in U.S. government, history, law, and democracy
- Incorporate discussion of current issues and events, particularly those important to young people, into the classroom
- Offer students the opportunity to perform community service, with the service-learning linked to academic lessons and the broader curriculum
- Encourage students to join extracurricular activities that get them involved in their schools or communities
- Give students a voice in the management of their own classrooms and schools

But if we have a pretty clear idea of how to teach the basics of good citizenship, what we still don't have—and haven't had for a long time—is a commitment to actually teaching them.

If our kids walk out of our school systems without an understanding of democracy, democracy will cease.

—Eighth-grade history teacher Dakota Draper

America's part in the Vietnam War had begun in earnest around the time my friends and I entered Merrick Avenue Junior High. It was still escalating when, six years later, we graduated from John F. Kennedy High School. Growing up with the war had politicized us. We'd heard the chants of "Hey, hey, LBJ, how many boys did you kill today?" We'd seen the grisly photos in *Life* magazine of the My Lai massacre. We'd learned that our government couldn't be trusted anymore to tell the truth.

Throughout high school, we'd become increasingly impatient with our classes for lacking, in a catchword of the era, "relevance." It frustrated us that while the world smoked and crackled like a burning hootch, we sat in Trigonometry class solving pointless problems or in English class parsing sample sentences. We wanted at least our graduation to be relevant, and so Neil, Dave, Andy, Steve, and I decided to wear black armbands to the ceremony as a protest against the war.

On graduation day some 500 seniors were lining up in the gym to march out to the football field when Mr. Witamak, a math teacher whose face always reminded me of a frog's, with bulgy eyes and wide, thin lips, began to shriek, "You can't wear that! You can't wear that!" He lunged at me and grabbed my armband and, after a moment's tussle, tore it off. Up and down the line, other teachers pounced on my friends.

We were shocked, outraged, humiliated—and at a loss about what to do next. But we knew we had to do something. The idea of a walkout took shape hurriedly as we sweated on wooden folding chairs on the blazing field, whispering back and forth across the rows.

"Should we do it?"

"I don't know. What do you think?"

"Let's do it."

"OK, we'll do it."

I'd be the first of us called up to receive his diploma. By the time they got to the Gs, my heart was trying to crash through my chest. I scanned the sun-scorched bleachers for my family. There they were. I wondered how my parents would react. My mouth felt as if it were packed with a thousand cotton balls.

The whole thing was over quickly. I heard my name and walked up the steps and across the stage. The school board president smiled at me and extended his hand in congratulations. I didn't shake it but thrust my arm high above my head and flashed the peace sign. Then I whirled on my heel and went down the steps. My friends rose from their chairs and marched off behind me to loud boos and scattered applause and with the hellish heat everywhere.

That was an important day in my civics education. But school didn't contribute to it except, perhaps, in a negative sense, as a blow to dodge or an obstacle to leap. The Westerns and World War II movies I grew up watching on TV—Gary Cooper in *High Noon*, Robert Taylor in *Bataan*—contributed more to my understanding of duty and honor and democracy. School was just something to endure, like a pain you hold your breath during to avoid screaming.

> *Skill to do comes of doing.*
>
> —Ralph Waldo Emerson

Of all the promising approaches to civics education mentioned in *The Civic Mission of Schools*, the most promising might be increasing students' control of their own schooling. Certainly, it's the most controversial, the only one not unanimously endorsed by the fifty-five experts who contributed to the report. Although some contributors argued that civics education works best when students have a voice in school governance, others doubted the need for fundamental changes in how schools operate or are organized. They didn't believe that a democratic ethos must permeate the culture of school for civics education to take hold. They believed that young people can learn democratic skills and attitudes quite as well in a prisonlike environment.[31]

But can they? A recent survey that found a majority of high school students are apathetic toward and ignorant of their First Amendment rights suggests not. Of the 112,000 students surveyed nationwide, 75 percent either didn't know how they felt about the First Amendment or admitted that they took it for granted. In addition, more than half erroneously believed that flag burning is illegal and that the government can censor the Internet, while a third thought that the First Amendment goes too far in the rights it guarantees.[32]

The indifference of most students to their constitutional rights can be blamed not only on poor classroom instruction—or what one curriculum director called the "deplorable situation" of civics education—but also on a lack of practice in exercising those rights.[33] Why would students value freedom of expression when they're rarely free to express themselves? How would they know it's important when they don't get to experience its importance firsthand? As a high school social studies teacher in Wisconsin said, "If we could involve the kids more in the decision-making at the school, where they see immediate impact and the ability to influence, that would put more of the message in them."[34]

School can't educate for democracy unless it operates to some extent as a democracy. Usually, of course, school operates more as a penitentiary. And that, cartoonist Terry Everton said in an article in *Z Magazine*, is "why school sucks." Everton, who was lumped in high school with "the outcast and the bored, the hopelessly fucked up," wrote that school "defines good citizens as

those who play by the rules, stay in line, and do as they're told."
School is designed not to foster curiosity or promote intellect, he
claimed, but to prepare people for "lifetimes of being pushed
around." Students are "threatened to either shape up, study
harder, quit daydreaming so damned much and get better grades
or begin practicing all the cool voice inflections you can use when
muttering, 'You want fries with that?'"[35]

Although stated more bluntly than usual, Everton's argument
that standardized education produces standardized people is
hardly new. John Dewey was making a version of it more than a
hundred years ago. But the argument has fresh urgency today
with the increased emphasis on standardized testing under the
No Child Left Behind Act. Everton's response to No Child Left
Behind, incidentally, was succinct: "No child left behind my
ass."[36]

Cursing out federal education legislation may be fun and ther-
apeutic, but it isn't likely to lead to the democratization of schooling. So what will? Some of the ideas that have been floated are
relatively simple, such as ensuring that student councils are "true
governments, not social clubs." Others are more audacious.
Richard Pratte, for example, suggested that teachers "must make
their classrooms miniature public spheres where the discourse of
democracy can be debated and where the issues that arise . . . can
be collectively and seriously evaluated." But simple or audacious,
the ideas all owe something to Dewey, who believed that students
are best prepared for democratic life by having actual experience
with democratic processes rather than by receiving isolated civic
lessons.[37]

Understand, no one is asking that adults abandon their posts
and leave the running of schools to the kids. All anyone is asking
is that teachers and administrators model democratic principles
by treating students with dignity and respect and that students be
involved—not in charge—in the way their schools are run.

Student involvement can mean many different things. It can mean allowing kindergartners to vote on which books to read at story time. It can mean encouraging older students to express their opinions about school policies and rules and to formulate solutions for school problems. It can mean developing a student bill of rights. It can mean organizing students into work crews to help with the maintenance of school buildings and grounds. It can mean inviting students to attend school board meetings or even to serve on school boards.[38]

The last is possible in New York State, where a law went into effect in 2003 that allows local school boards to appoint a high school student as a nonvoting member. Having a student serve alongside the adult members is supposed to fill two purposes—first, provide boards with the student perspective on issues, and, second, provide students, at least those few who are appointed, with an important lesson in civics.[39]

So far it hasn't quite worked out that way, not because the law is flawed or the student representatives aren't trying but because, until now, the students had zero practice in democratic discourse. As a result, they often feel as shaken and distraught during board meetings as dogs do during thunderstorms. Finally they get the opportunity to have a say in their own education, and what happens? They discover that they haven't the necessary training to take advantage of it.

The boy who serves as the student representative on my local school board admitted in an interview to feeling intimidated by the adult members. "I have to overcome that to bring up some of the views [of students]," he acknowledged. "If there is something being said that I don't agree with, I'm going to start talking out more before they ask me."[40] Good for him. But it won't be easy, not after twelve years of school throughout which he and his classmates have been told to sit down, shut up, and listen.

To me, the most radical of all American ideas is that everyone can be educated—not just that everyone can go to school, but that everyone can be educated.

—Diane Ravitch

Civics education may seem thin and frail, a sick old woman attached to a feeding tube, but there are signs that the patient is rallying. Only recently

- The Bush administration, pointing to embarrassing student stumbles over the Pledge of Allegiance and the Gettysburg Address, convened a We the People White House Forum on American History, Civics, and Service to brainstorm solutions to the problem.[41]
- Congress passed the American History and Civics Act, which would establish twelve centers at colleges and universities around the country to provide improved training for American history and civics teachers.[42]
- The Corporation for Public Broadcasting announced plans to help teach students American history and civics by incorporating public television with other media, especially the Internet. "[We]'re hoping to reach kids wherever they are learning," a spokeswoman said. "That might include schools, libraries, after-school programs, or at home."[43]

Meanwhile, public support for civics education is running strong, even among young people, who as a group tend to shun politics. A 2002 survey of fifteen- to twenty-five-year-olds found that 66 percent favored the idea of mandatory civics classes in middle school and high school. Another survey found that nine out of ten Americans say it's important for high schools to teach civics and government.[44]

Surveys are further finding that civics education actually increases students' civic knowledge, skills, and engagement. Those who report that they chose to take a civics or government class are more likely than other young people to also report that they helped solve a community problem, made consumer decisions for ethical or political reasons, believe in the importance of voting, and are registered to vote.[45]

Despite these hopeful signs, it'd be a mistake to assume that the patient—or democracy—is out of danger. Policymakers may make concerned noises about the feeble condition of the body politic, but they don't often act all that concerned. In 2003, the U.S. Department of Education spent less than half of 1 percent of its total budget on civics education.[46]

Attempts to revive civics education face other obstacles beyond just a lack of funding. For one thing, the current national fixation with high-stakes testing of math and reading draws time and attention away from social studies in general and civics in particular. For another, many teachers fear criticism or even lawsuits if they discuss controversial topics in class, though research shows that such discussions stimulate student interest in politics and social issues.[47]

Clearly, schools aren't yet the kind of places that ignite in young people what Jefferson called "the sacred fire of freedom and self-government." Quite the opposite. The more docile students are, the better teachers and school administrators like it. But if educators don't kindle Jefferson's sacred fire, who will? Elected officials? Families? The media? It has been remarked that "while the work of preparing citizens for democracy must include more than the schools, the schools are the public institution best positioned to affect the vast majority of young people."[48] Schools can set minds ablaze or, as now, despite night falling and the wolves prowling all around, let the fire go out.

NOTES

1. Cynthia Gibson and Peter Levine, *The Civic Mission of Schools* (New York: CIRCLE and Carnegie Corporation, 2003), 19.
2. J. Martin Rochester, "The Training of Idiots," in *Where Did Social Studies Go Wrong?*, ed. James Leming, Lucien Ellington, and Kathleen Porter (Dayton, Ohio: Thomas B. Fordham Foundation, 2003), 6.
3. Gibson and Levine, *The Civic Mission of Schools*, 5, 14–15; Charles N. Quigley, "Civic Education: Recent History, Current Status, and the Future," http://www.itd-amherst.org/RCE/historyciviced.html (accessed November 19, 2004); "From Classroom to Citizen: American Attitudes on Civic Education" (Calabasas, Calif.: Center for Civic Education, 2004), 4.
4. "Quick Facts," http://www.civicyouth.org/quick.civic_ed.htm (accessed December 28, 2004); Rod Paige, "Civics Education in America," *Phi Delta Kappan*, September 2003, 59.
5. Ben Feller, "Don't Know Much about History," sfgate.com, http://www.sfgate.com/cgi-bin/article.cgi?file+/news/archive/2003/07/02/national1510E... (accessed November 29, 2004); Rochester, "The Training of Idiots," 10.
6. Quigley, "Civic Education."
7. Quigley, "Civic Education."
8. Quoted in Anne Turnbaugh Lockwood, "Educating for Democracy," *Leaders for Tomorrow's Schools*, spring 1997, 16.
9. Quigley, "Civic Education."
10. Quigley, "Civic Education."
11. This anecdote is recounted in Feller, "Don't Know Much about History."
12. Gibson and Levine, *The Civic Mission of Schools*, 11; Quigley, "Civic Education."
13. "From Classroom to Citizen," 10.
14. For a summary of Jefferson's efforts on behalf of education, see Sarah Mondale and Sarah B. Patton, eds., *School: The Story of American Public Education* (Boston: Beacon Press, 2001), 23–25.
15. Mondale and Patton, *School*, 72; Quigley, "Civic Education"; Emma Lazarus, "The New Colossus," in *101 Great American Poems* (New

York: Dover, 1998), 33; quoted in Jeffrey Mirel, "The Decline of Civic Education," *Daedalus*, summer 2002, 51.

16. Quigley, "Civic Education."

17. Quigley, "Civic Education."

18. Quigley, "Civic Education"; Gibson and Levine, *The Civic Mission of Schools*, 6.

19. Quoted in Nel Noddings, "Renewing Democracy in School," *Phi Delta Kappan*, April 1999, 579.

20. Rochester, "The Training of Idiots," 10

21. Feller, "Don't Know Much about History."

22. Rochester, "The Training of Idiots," 7.

23. Joseph Kahane and Joel Westheimer, "Teaching Democracy: What Schools Need to Do," *Phi Delta Kappan*, September 2003, 35.

24. "From Classroom to Citizen," 6.

25. Kahane and Westheimer, "Teaching Democracy," 36.

26. Joel Westheimer and Joseph Kahane, "Reconnecting Education to Democracy: Democratic Dialogues," *Phi Delta Kappan*, September 2003, 10.

27. Quoted in Lockwood, "Educating for Democracy," 16; Roger Soder, "The Good Citizen and the Common School," *Phi Delta Kappan*, September 2003, 37; Melissa K. Comber, "Civics Curriculum and Civic Skills: Recent Evidence," http://www.civicyouth.org (accessed February 5, 2005); Richard Pratte, *The Civic Imperative* (New York: Teachers College Press, 1988), 2.

28. Pratte, *The Civic Imperative*, 21; Kahane and Westheimer, "Teaching Democracy," 39–40; Noddings, "Renewing Democracy in School," 579.

29. Pratte, *The Civic Imperative*, 8; Soder, "Good Citizen," 37.

30. Gibson and Levine, *The Civic Mission of Schools*, 6, 27.

31. Gibson and Levine, *The Civic Mission of Schools*, 16, 31.

32. Jessica L. Tonn, "First Amendment Attitudes Found Troubling," *Education Week*, February 2, 2005, 6.

33. Quoted in Tonn, "First Amendment Attitudes Found Troubling."

34. Quoted in Feller, "Don't Know Much about History."

35. Terry Everton, "Why School Sucks," *Z Magazine*, November 2004, 54–56.

36. Everton, "Why School Sucks," 55.

37. Feller, "Don't Know Much about History"; Pratte, *The Civic Imperative*, 14; Noddings, "Renewing Democracy in School," 579.

38. See Shara Ahmad-Llewellyn, "From Knowledge, to Service, to Citizenship," *Phi Delta Kappan*, September 2003, 62; Noddings, "Renewing Democracy in School," 579; Gibson and Levine, *The Civic Mission of Schools*, 31.

39. Associated Press, "School Boards Now Open to Students," *Poughkeepsie* (N.Y.) *Journal*, August 10, 2003, 7A.

40. Quoted in Andrew Hackmack, "Senior Brings Student Voice to School Board," *Southern Ulster Times*, January 5, 2004, 5.

41. Paige, "Civics Education in America," 59; Feller, "Don't Know Much about History."

42. Feller, "Don't Know Much about History."

43. Associated Press, "Groups Make Plans to Build Better Citizens," http://famulus.msnbc.com/famulusgen/ap12-03-09400.asp?t+ap-news&vts+12320041017 (accessed December 3, 2004).

44. Gibson and Levine, *The Civic Mission of Schools*, 12; "Quick Facts"; Quigley, "Civic Education."

45. Comber, "Civics Curriculum and Civic Skills"; Peter Levine and Mark Hugo Lopez, "Themes Emphasized in Social Studies and Civics Classes: New Evidence," http://www.civicyouth.org (accessed February 5, 2005).

46. Kahane and Westheimer, "Teaching Democracy," 34–35.

47. Gibson and Levine, *The Civic Mission of Schools*, 15.

48. Westheimer and Kahane, "Reconnecting Education to Democracy," 4.

4

THOSE WHO CAN'T

I feel a tightness in my chest that makes it hard to breathe. My jaw throbs as if someone just punched me there. A wave of nausea washes over me. I break out in a cold sweat.

This can mean only one of two things: either I'm having a heart attack or Darla is talking again at dinner about becoming a teacher when she grows up.

Why such an adverse reaction to her choice of career? Could it possibly be because, according to some estimates, half of all new teachers leave teaching within five years?[1] Yeah, it could.

I mention to a friend my misgivings about Darla growing up to be a teacher. My friend looks at me in surprise. "But you're a teacher!" she exclaims.

Precisely.

• • •

My feelings about teaching are complicated—too complicated to fit on a coffee mug or a T-shirt ("I touch the future; I teach."). I know teaching is a noble profession. I also know it can be a horribly frustrating one.

CHAPTER 4

It isn't just that we're underpaid, underappreciated, and under suspicion. It isn't just that we're hemmed in by numerous niggling rules and policies and the impenetrable acronyms of the latest educational jargon. It isn't just that we're supposed to somehow clean up the mess made of kids by the rest of society. Rather, it's all these things, each of which taken separately might be tolerable but which, like pills and booze, are lethal in combination.

• • •

So what do you tell a bright young woman who says she wants to be a teacher? If you're a teacher yourself, the battle-scarred veteran of years of class warfare, perhaps you tell her to pick another career.

That at least is what Ismene Siteles told Esmé Raji Codell when Codell was her student teacher. "You're a very gifted teacher," Siteles said. "Don't teach. Be an actress instead." It was advice that Codell later found herself wishing she had taken as she struggled to cope with hostile administrators, apathetic colleagues, and inner-city fifth graders during her first year of teaching.[2]

Then there's high school English teacher Brendan Halpin, who, after one of his best students, Diane, said she wanted to be a teacher, was strongly tempted to warn her against it. As he explains in his memoir, *Losing My Faculties*, "At one time I thought that if more people like Diane went into teaching, the profession would become more respectable and schools would get more functional." But now he's not so sure. "I no longer think I can change it," he says, "and I guess I kind of doubt she can either."[3]

I know the feeling. When Darla says she wants to be a teacher, my heart shrivels. I look at her energy and intelligence, her beautiful potential, and all I can think is, "Christ, what a waste."

• • •

The kind of people who used to go into teaching—that is, "high-aptitude" women—don't generally go into it anymore. They can now go into better-paying, more prestigious professions, such as medicine, engineering, finance, and law. Teacher educator Theodore R. Sizer was only half joking when he recently remarked, "We could solve the teacher quality problem overnight. All we have to do is take away all opportunities for women to have other jobs."[4]

An increasing share of the teaching ranks are filled today by women from bottom-tier colleges who scored poorly on achievement tests. One study found that college graduates whose SAT or ACT scores were in the bottom quartile were more than twice as likely as those in the top quartile to have majored in education.[5] The education majors I encounter—a couple take my basic newswriting course every semester in the mistaken belief that journalism is fun and easy—tend to be unimpressive. They rarely participate in class discussions or keep up with assigned readings or follow the news, and, what's worse, they often act offended if I suggest they should.

"Quality education begins with quality teaching," Vivian Troen and Katherine C. Boles write in *Who's Teaching Your Children?*, "but teaching is a job that fewer and fewer people of quality want to do." In their opinion, teacher quality is lower now than at any time since the era of the one-room schoolhouse.[6]

We've all heard the old saying, "Those who can, do; those who can't, teach." Unfortunately, the old saying may have new validity.

● ● ●

After finishing *Educating Esmé*, Codell's diary of her first year of teaching, I gave it to Darla to read. "You'll like this," I said, placing the book on her makeup-cluttered dresser. I secretly hoped that it might cause her to rethink her career plans. Although Codell emerges in its pages as smart, dedicated, and funny, other teachers emerge as monsters of mediocrity—negative, timid, and uninspired.

Negative. In the days before school opens, Codell excitedly sets up her classroom. There's a bulletin board with a red schoolhouse shape and the caption, "New School . . . You're What

Makes It Special." There's a smiley-faced mobile of "Kind Words." There's a spelling center with spelling games, a typewriter, an electric wiggle pencil, a box of cornmeal, and sponge letters with tempera paint. There's a learning center with flags of all nations. Codell thinks the classroom looks beautiful and feels sorry for any kid not in it, but the older teachers just shake their heads. They "told me my room looked overstimulating."[7]

Timid. Codell often clashes with the school principal, Mr. Turner, a pompous, self-promoting "educrat." Her willingness to challenge his authority for the sake of her class frightens the other teachers, who, rather than support her, beg her to shut up. "Don't make him angry—you know he'll just take it out on us," they say, and "Stop being so confrontational; you're bringing down morale."[8]

Uninspired. As horrible as Codell finds this, she finds faculty meetings even more so. She describes a typical agenda: "lines and keeping children in them, the proliferation of talking and how to stop it, textbooks and state goals, are all the children learning what everyone else is learning?" The meetings are enough to convince her that a conspiracy must exist to make children's days as boring and meaningless as possible.[9]

It seems to me that a father might be forgiven for trying to save his youngest daughter from a future full of meetings like these.

• • •

The numbers concerning teaching are grim. In September 2000, the average starting salary for teachers was $26,845, compared with $33,143 in sales, $37,255 in public accounting, and $49,111 in chemical engineering[10]—which explains, I guess, why 58 percent of teachers take a second job outside school.[11]

But if you think that's bad—can you imagine any other professional, a doctor or lawyer or engineer, having to moonlight as a bartender at Applebee's in order to make ends meet—consider this:

- Seventy-five percent of potential teachers who begin an undergraduate teaching program leave the profession before their first year of teaching.[12]
- About 30 percent of new teachers leave the profession after three years, and more than 45 percent leave after five years. It's precisely those schools that can least afford to lose teachers, low-performing schools in high-poverty areas, that lose the most.[13]
- Teachers work an average of forty-nine hours a week, eleven of which are uncompensated.[14]
- The average teacher spends $408 of his or her own money a year on books, stickers, and other supplies.[15] When Donna Moffett began teaching at P.S. 92 in Brooklyn in 2000, she was advised to have a basket of bathroom supplies—soap, paper towels, even toilet paper—in her classroom at all times because the school bathrooms were so rarely stocked with them.[16]

"School reform will go nowhere," Troen and Boles write, "and the quality of public education will be no better than mediocre until a parent is able to say, 'My child is going to be a teacher' with the same pride of accomplishment as 'My child is going to be a doctor.'"[17] Having seen the numbers, I'm not likely to say that anytime soon.

• • •

School districts face a shortage of 2.2 million teachers over the next decade. The shortage is largely the result of two converging demographic trends: increasing student enrollments and increasing numbers of teachers reaching retirement age.[18] But compounding the problem is teacher attrition. That is, recruiting new teachers isn't a solution when 40 to 50 percent quit within a few short years.

The teacher shortage has sometimes been compared to a bucket rapidly losing water because of holes in the bottom. "Pouring more water in the bucket," one pair of researchers pointed out, "will not do any good if we do not patch the holes first."[19]

But a more apt comparison may be to the Battle of the Somme, July 1, 1916, during which the British suffered 60,000 casualties, of whom 21,000 were killed, most in the first hour of the attack, perhaps the first minutes. One battalion after another stepped out into no-man's-land that morning in France to be swept away by a tornado of German machine-gun fire.[20]

Why didn't the British high command do something about it? Why did they let the attack go on? Military historian John Keegan blamed in part the spirit of World War I generalship, which believed in the inevitability of heavy casualties.[21] Schools, sad to say, seem to be run according to the same gruesome philosophy.

• • •

While doctors serve long residencies and lawyers may work for years under senior partners, new teachers are left on their own to sink or swim.

Many sink.

"We've not done a good job of creating entry conditions to help them learn their job well," admits Pat Wasley, dean of the University of Washington's College of Education in Seattle. "We have to acknowledge them as novices."[22] But, instead, new teachers are often given the worst schedules and the toughest students, all the screw-ups and misfits no one else wants to teach.[23] And so it's with a shiver of horror that most teachers recall their first year of teaching, when they were nervous and raw and received little or no support from parents, administrators, or colleagues.

Anita S. Coleman, who started her teaching career at an inner-city school in New Jersey: "I was filled with constant frustration and exhaustion. I found myself faced unmercifully with my own limitations. I yelled often, for I didn't know how else to relieve the stress caused by the incredible energy of the youngsters. Sometimes I wasn't even aware that I had been yelling."[24]

Andrew Dean Mullen, who started his teaching career at an elementary school in Colorado: "By three o'clock each day the room was a mess and I was a wreck. . . . Papers to be graded, charts to be updated, and forms to be sent to the office mushroomed everywhere. Teachers' magazines I'd once devoured eagerly began to gather dust."[25]

Lisa M. Shipley, who started her teaching career at a middle school in Missouri: "College did not prepare me for the student whose mother was murdered by a jealous boyfriend; for the student who witnessed a drive-by shooting; for the student who was removed from her home because of an abusive father."[26]

Ron Wolfson, who started his teaching career at a high school in the Bronx: "There was no textbook and the only aid I was given was a book of lesson plans from the mid-1960s, which besides being hopelessly out of date was for students with greater skills than those of my kids. . . . A totally exhausting experience that first year, teaching usually left me fast asleep before ten o'-clock on Friday nights, my reward for making it through another week."[27]

Elizabeth Gold, who started her teaching career at an alternative school in Jackson Heights, Queens: "I grew to hate . . . Room 313, with its computer screens and its sour human smell and the one window too high and too small for anyone to jump out of. . . . [I]f I have any luck, I'll never walk into that damn room again."[28]

Taken together, these voices speaking about the first year of teaching form a chorus of heartbreak, a kind of dirge, an immense and inconsolable wailing.

CHAPTER 4

•••

People just seem to expect new teachers to suck it up. Even new teachers themselves expect to be able to suck it up. That, after all, is what new teachers do in movies. They don't whine or burn out or quit. They suck it up.

In the 1967 movie *To Sir, with Love*, an inexperienced black teacher, played by Sidney Poitier, is assigned to a class of white kids bearing all the stigmata of the London slums. "Most of our students are rejects from other schools. . . ," the principal warns him, and adds, "From the moment you accept this position, you'll be entirely on your own." Does this discourage him? Does it drive him away? There would be no movie if it did. Although an engineer by training, he manages to reach kids the veteran teachers have written off. "You really are getting involved with your children," an astonished colleague says, to which he replies, "I'm just trying to help. That's the job, isn't it?" Indeed it is, and he achieves such satisfying results with students that when he finally gets offered work as an engineer, he passes it up to stay at this crap hole of a school.

A more recent movie, *Dangerous Minds* from 1995, tells the same basic story, except now the teacher is white and the students are black. The teacher is also a woman (Michelle Pfeiffer), not to mention an ex-Marine (Michelle Pfeiffer!). At first, she can't control the class—"Who are these kids," she plaintively asks another teacher, "rejects from hell?"—but then draws on her military background to whip them into academic shape. Apparently, it doesn't hurt her teaching effectiveness either that she wears a cool leather jacket and has good cheekbones.

These and a couple of other movies are what might be called "in spite of" stories. By that I mean the movies show new teachers succeeding in spite of all the obstacles in their way, including crumbling school buildings, lack of administrative and parental support, racial prejudice, and their own doubts and inexperience.

The movies hold out the promise that a determined teacher can go, in the words of one of the movies' titles, *Up the Down Staircase*—can counteract or at least transcend total system failure.[29] It's a reaffirmation of the old American faith in the efficacy of individual effort. It's also borderline ridiculous.

No matter. Teachers have fallen for it. Elizabeth Gold, who left teaching after a year in a big, urban high school, wondered in retrospect, "Had I seen one too many movies? Did I imagine surging violins?"[30] Donna Moffett certainly imagined them. Before she began teaching, she was enthralled by movies like *To Sir, with Love* and *Dangerous Minds*, whose teacher-heroes are a combination of truant officers, social workers, and fairy godparents. But once she became a teacher herself, she quickly realized that she'd been hoodwinked. She couldn't live up to the standards Hollywood established for teachers. No one but Sidney Poitier or Michelle Pfeiffer could.[31]

Brendan Halpin would make the same rude discovery his first year of teaching. His students got high in school regularly, but rather than try to help them, he looked the other way. It was easier.

"So much," he recalled with a sigh, "for my heroic-teacher movie."[32]

• • •

Researchers have compiled a long list of reasons why teachers say they quit. Many cite low salaries, but even more complain about poor working conditions.[33] Troen and Boles contend in their book *Who's Teaching Your Children?* that teachers endure "the worst working conditions of any so-called professional."[34] Most have no telephones, no fax machines, no personal computers, and only limited access to copiers. "We weren't allowed to use the copy machine [for handouts]," Sue Manley, a former fourth-grade teacher on the South Side of Chicago, recounted, "so I had to stop at Kinko's every morning on my way to work. There was never any toilet paper in the bathroom for the kids, so I had to bring that, too."[35]

The very buildings in which teachers work can be an obstacle to job satisfaction. Bel Kaufman's description of a fictional but typical urban high school, Calvin Coolidge, is as depressingly accurate today as it was when she wrote it more than forty years ago: "cracked plaster, broken windows, splintered doors and carved up desks, gloomy corridors, metal stairways, dingy cafeteria."[36] The National Education Association estimates that 60 percent of all schools in America are in need of major repairs.[37]

Another reason teachers give for leaving is little to no administrative support. Jim Treman, a California teacher who quit after two years, said, "I was promised a ton of support, which in the end turned out to be completely untrue. I was totally alone."[38] Almost two-thirds of former teachers in North Carolina indicated in a survey that a lack of administrative support was a factor in their leaving.[39]

Still other teachers quit out of fear for their safety. Esmé Raji Codell, who eventually left classroom teaching to become a school librarian, taught in a neighborhood plagued by gangs and drug-related violence. "Will I be shot by a student?" she used to wonder. "So many of them have guns at home. Why will I be shot? For suspending, scolding, letting someone cut in line, for giving too much homework?"[40] The breaking point came for Sue Manley, the fourth-grade teacher who frequented Kinko's, when she read a student's journal entry that described violent acts directed at her.[41]

Teachers also say they leave because they feel inadequately prepared for the pressures of teaching, because they're inundated with extracurricular duties, because they're assigned to the most-difficult-to-teach students or to courses outside their areas of expertise, because they have few opportunities for advancement, and because they suffer from loneliness and isolation.[42] Given all this, perhaps the question to ask isn't why so many teachers leave but why any of them stay.

• • •

Or, what's to be done about the epidemic loss of teachers, particularly new teachers? Private industry takes high employee turnover seriously because of its costs, not only in terms of dollars but also in terms of productivity and morale.[43] Teacher turnover should be taken just as seriously by school districts and for much the same reasons.

Each teacher who leaves costs a district $11,000 to replace. Nationwide, teacher turnover is estimated to cost a staggering $5.8 billion in termination, recruitment, and training expenses.[44] Now add in the harm done to students by having an unstable and largely inexperienced cast of teachers, and the costs become even more exorbitant.

Good thing, then, that most of the issues underlying teacher turnover are what the experts call "policy amenable," meaning that the issues aren't inevitable or irreparable but can be addressed through specific policy changes.[45] And so, if teachers are leaving because of low pay, change policy to pay them more. If they're leaving because of inadequate administrative support or feelings of loneliness and isolation, change policy to assign them mentors. If they're leaving because of fear for their own safety, change policy to protect them from potentially dangerous students.

Clearly, none of this is impossible to do. It's just, under present circumstances, pretty unlikely.

• • •

As someone who served six years on a school board, including (oy vey!) three as president, I know from experience that boards are rarely sympathetic to the plight of teachers. And even if they were sympathetic, they would still have too little money to do much about it. School budgets are a desperate balancing act, and, frankly, more plates end up smashed on the floor than merrily spinning, to general applause, on the nimble fingertips of antic board members.

I'm not saying there aren't attempts to address the problem of teacher turnover. There are. Increasingly, states and districts have mandated, for example, mentoring programs that pair novices with experienced teachers. Some of these programs actually work well, though many more don't. A survey by Harvard University's Project on the Next Generation of Teachers found that mentors seldom provide the help most new teachers imagine they will— "personal encouragement, assistance in curriculum development, advice about lesson plans, and feedback about teaching." Rather, the pairings are often inappropriate (different subjects, grades, or even schools), and personalities don't always click.[46]

My own district has been reluctant to fund a mentoring program (so what that it's a new state law?). The current board president, who bears a disconcerting resemblance to Charlie Brown, even down to the squiggle of hair, has argued at meetings that experienced teachers shouldn't be paid to serve as mentors but should do it for free out of duty to their profession. This is a curious argument, one that makes teaching sound like joining a monastery or signing up for a suicide mission, which some teachers, having to endure inadequate pay and unmotivated students and now his crap, must feel it kind of is.

It would be hard to exaggerate the antiteacher sentiment that exists on most school boards. I used to cringe at the slurs my fellow board members would let drop about our teachers, how they were selfish and stupid and lazy and had gone into teaching because they couldn't hack the private sector. Granted, my district is somewhat retrograde, Mayberry without the folksy charm, but to one degree or another the same negative stereotype of teachers darkens other districts.

The truth is, many people don't see teaching as real work, like, say, polluting the environment or raiding the stock market. Although teachers typically have heavy workloads—a "high school

assignment may include 150 students, several course prepara-
tions, hall duty each day, and meetings after school"[47]—there per-
sists the perception that they rarely overexert themselves. Perhaps it stems from the fact that teachers have summers off or that
teaching is predominantly a female profession. Or perhaps teachers are resented just for being teachers.

Back when I was on the school board, a constituent, an old man
with rheumy eyes who was commander of the local VFW, called
my house one evening with a suggestion for saving the district
money. Why not replace social studies teachers with the History
Channel? The programs on it, he said, are excellent.

I laughed into the phone. I couldn't help it. A friend of mine always referred to the History Channel as the Hitler Channel. I suddenly had this mental picture of high school students slumped in
semidarkness as a TV played black-and-white archival footage
from World War II and a melodramatic narrator solemnized
about the Beer Hall Putsch and the Eagle's Nest and blonde Nazi
bombshell Eva Braun.

But I shouldn't have laughed. I should've taken the old man seriously. Although I didn't realize it at the time, he was expressing
a common belief that teachers are nothing special, little more, in
fact, than overpaid babysitters, easy enough to replace with TV
or, as it has turned out, a regime of annual standardized testing.

● ● ●

There's zero guarantee that the No Child Left Behind Act—or, as its
critics have sarcastically redubbed it, the "Leave No Child Untested
Act"—will make for better teachers or better students. It might actually make for worse. But it does guarantee that teachers will be
under tighter control and closer scrutiny. Now if a topic isn't likely
to be on one of the new, federally mandated state tests, it doesn't
get taught. Teachers must stick to the curriculum as designed by
state ed; otherwise, their students' test scores may suffer. And test

scores are everything—compared among districts, analyzed for patterns, publicized in newspapers.

Is someone who's told what to teach and how to teach it and then does just as he or she has been told truly a teacher? Isn't that like calling a monkey or dog orbiting the Earth in a space capsule an astronaut? The whole goal of No Child Left Behind seems to be to eliminate local variety and individual idiosyncrasy and make the teacher a kind of automaton, a poor, hapless dog in a spacesuit. Would Darla still want to teach if she knew she couldn't set the course, work the controls, or look out the porthole and see unfamiliar stars? Would you?

• • •

I hear Darla singing. The door to her room is closed, but I can hear her behind it trying out a Gershwin classic, "Someone to Watch Over Me." She has a lovely voice, full of vibrato, as if she were pulsing with adult emotions.

This is all a bit surprising. Darla has belonged to chorus since fourth grade, but almost indifferently, the way most people belong to a book club. Then the high school hired a new chorus teacher, a young woman recently out of college, who noticed Darla hidden among the altos and praised her voice and encouraged her to refine it.

Now Darla hangs out in the chorus room during lunch period and after school, and when she comes home, she practices her songs without having to be reminded. At dinner she doesn't ever talk about Earth Science or English, unless it's to complain that there's a test or a lot of homework, but she's always chattering about the song selections for the spring concert and who's up for a solo and what Ms. Ruiz, the chorus teacher, said.

It's nice that Darla has found at least one thing at school to get excited about. It must be nice for the chorus teacher, too. Without Darla and some other kids like her, school would probably be unbearable for Ms. Ruiz, a tedious hell of discipline problems and cafeteria duty and paperwork to fill out.

Bel Kaufman perfectly captured in *Up the Down Staircase*, her novel that was the basis for the movie, the kind of small victories on which a teacher's sanity can depend. Its narrator, first-year teacher Sylvia Barrett, says, "Whenever I feel too frustrated to go on, I find an unexpected compensation: a girl whose face lights up when she enters the room; a boy who begins making sense out of words on a printed page; or a class that groans in dismay when the end-of-period bell rings."[48] These are what are sometimes called "the intrinsic rewards of teaching." Intrinsic rewards are necessary because teaching has so few extrinsic ones—you know, like money or status.

• • •

The student, a graduating senior, gave me a chunk of crystal with a quote from Henry Adams etched on it: "A Teacher Affects Eternity. He Can Never Tell Where His Influence Stops." She gave it to me mostly as a thank-you, but also, she said, to remind me not to lose hope when my classes seemed hopeless.

Good teaching is hard work. It may look easy, like any dimwit can do it, but not any dimwit can. You've got to concentrate, and you've got to prepare, and perhaps you've got to have an inborn talent, the soul of an artist.

As a young man, I had no intention of making a career out of teaching. I wanted to be a writer, and teaching just seemed more sensible than stealing car stereos to support my twice-a-day writing habit. But a teacher is what I've primarily become, at least according to my income tax returns. On the line that asks my occupation, the accountant doesn't put Writer-Teacher. He puts Teacher-Writer.

Most days I can live with that.

Other people sell kids' stuff that's ugly or unnecessary or that may hurt them, either now or twenty years from now. Other people exploit them, scare them, pack them off to war. I don't. I teach them.

Of course, I can't always find the right key to unlock their curiosity about a subject. I search my key ring, my painfully acquired set of classroom skills, but the key may not be there, or, if it is, I may not recognize it. When that happens, I brood and fret and feel like the world's worst failure.

But when the key fits, oh, wow.

It doesn't matter then that the classroom clock is broken or that there aren't enough books to go around. It doesn't matter that the state keeps changing the curriculum or that the department chair has the ethics of a cannibal. It doesn't even matter that the pay is bad. All that matters is that a teacher is asking questions and that the students are asking questions back, learning to think for themselves, and finding out that it's not only important but also—just look at the sparkle in their eyes!—a joy.

NOTES

1. Theodore R. Sizer, *The Red Pencil: Convictions from Experience in Education* (New Haven, Conn.: Yale University Press, 2004), 47.

2. Esmé Raji Codell, *Educating Esmé: Diary of a Teacher's First Year* (Chapel Hill, N.C.: Algonquin Books of Chapel Hill, 1999), 15.

3. Brendan Halpin, *Losing My Faculties: A Teacher's Story* (New York: Villard, 2003), 236–37.

4. Quoted in Vivian Troen and Katherine C. Boles, *Who's Teaching Your Children?* (New Haven, Conn.: Yale University Press, 2003), 34–35.

5. Abby Goodnough, *Ms. Moffett's First Year: Becoming a Teacher in America* (New York: Public Affairs, 2004), 28. See also Teresa Mendez, "How Do the New Teachers Measure Up?" *Christian Science Monitor*, March 8, 2005, 11.

6. Troen and Boles, *Who's Teaching Your Children?*, 15, 16.

7. Codell, *Educating Esmé*, 23–25.

8. Codell, *Educating Esmé*, 114.

9. Codell, *Educating Esmé*, 116.

10. Goodnough, *Ms. Moffett's First Year*, 27.

11. Troen and Boles, *Who's Teaching Your Children?*, 62.

12. "Literature Review: Teacher Attrition/Retention," *Oregon Research Report*, April 2002, unpaged.

13. Claudia Graziano, "School's Out," *Edutopia*, February/March 2005, 40.

14. Troen and Boles, *Who's Teaching Your Children?*, 65.

15. Troen and Boles, *Who's Teaching Your Children?*, 65.

16. Goodnough, *Ms. Moffett's First Year*, 23.

17. Troen and Boles, *Who's Teaching Your Children?*, 81.

18. Susan Moore Johnson and Sarah E. Birkeland, "Pursuing 'a Sense of Success': New Teachers Explain Their Career Decisions" (online version of a paper prepared for the Annual Meeting of the American Educational Research Association, New Orleans, April 1–5, 2002), 1.

19. Richard M. Ingersoll and Thomas M. Smith, "Keeping Good Teachers," *Educational Leadership*, May 2003, 30–33. See also Seth Stern, "The Great Escape," *Christian Science Monitor*, October 7, 2003, 13, where Tom Carroll, executive director of the National Commission on Teaching and America's Future, is quoted as saying, "We have a bucket with huge holes in it. They're leaving as fast as we pour them in."

20. John Keegan, *The Face of Battle* (New York: Viking Press, 1976), 255.

21. Keegan, *The Face of Battle*, 256–57.

22. Quoted in Stern, "The Great Escape," 13.

23. Troen and Boles, *Who's Teaching Your Children?*, 65–66; Graziano, "School's Out," 40.

24. Anita S. Charles, "It Say, I'm Very Mad at You," in *My First Year as a Teacher*, ed. Pearl Rock Kane (New York: Signet, 1992), 81.

25. Andrew Dean Mullen, "Order in the Classroom," in Kane, *My First Year as a Teacher*, 70.

26. Quoted in Amy DePaul, *What to Expect Your First Year of Teaching* (Washington, D.C.: U.S. Department of Education, 1998), 18.

27. Ron Wolfson, "Graduation," in Kane, *My First Year as a Teacher*, 157–58.

28. Elizabeth Gold, *Brief Intervals of Horrible Sanity: One Season in a Progressive School* (New York: Tarcher, 2003), 8–9.

29. The movie, released in 1967 and starring Sandy Dennis, was based on Bel Kaufman's best-selling 1963 novel of the same name.

30. Gold, *Brief Intervals of Horrible Sanity*, 10.

31. Goodnough, *Ms. Moffett's First Year*, 160–61.

32. Halpin, *Losing My Faculties*, 41.

33. Ingersoll and Smith, "Keeping Good Teachers," 30–33.

34. Troen and Boles, *Who's Teaching Your Children?*, 63–64.

35. Quoted in Graziano, "School's Out," 41–42.

36. Bel Kaufman, *Up the Down Staircase* (Englewood Cliffs, N.J.: Prentice Hall, 1963), 32.

37. Troen and Boles, *Who's Teaching Your Children?*, 64.

38. Quoted in Graziano, "School's Out," 42. Brendan Halpin, who started his teaching career in Newcastle, Massachusetts, recalled that one ten-minute class visit from the vice principal "constituted the entirety of my supervision in my first year of teaching." Halpin, *Losing My Faculties*, 49.

39. Bridget Curran and Liam Goldrick, "Issue Brief: Mentoring and Supporting New Teachers," Education Policy Studies Division, National Governors Association for Best Practices, January 9, 2002, 2.

40. Codell, *Educating Esmé*, 152.

41. Graziano, "School's Out," 42.

42. "Literature Review."

43. Ingersoll and Smith, "Keeping Good Teachers," 30–33; Stern, "The Great Escape," 13.

44. Graziano, "School's Out," 40; Stern, "The Great Escape," 13.

45. Cassandra Guarino, Lucrecia Santibanez, Glenn Daley, and Dominic Brewer, "A Review of the Literature on Teacher Recruitment and Retention," Rand Corporation, May 2004, xi; Ingersoll and Smith, "Keeping Good Teachers," 30–33.

46. Johnson and Birkeland, "Pursuing 'a Sense of Success,'" 42.

47. Johnson and Birkeland, "Pursuing 'a Sense of Success,'" 42.

48. Kaufman, *Up the Down Staircase*, 242.

5

BOARD TO DEATH

It was once a crime in England to live more than a month with gypsies.

Really.

I bring this up because it's the kind of archaic policy that school boards sometimes adopt. In 2002, the school board in Cobb County, Georgia, apparently determined to return its district to the Middle Ages, voted to place stickers on science textbooks saying, "Evolution is a theory, not a fact, regarding the origin of living things."

What's next? Mandating that students wear garlic around their necks to ward off vampires?

Let me be clear. I don't doubt the sincerity or dedication of most school board members. I just doubt their competence.

In my own district, the school board recently voted against accepting a grant—the equivalent of "free money"—to replace the old card catalog at the high school library with a computerized system. "Nobody's taking books out of this library anyway," one board member said.

And he's considered the intellectual of the group.

• • •

It's now two years since I last served on the school board, and I don't want to go back to it, ever.

I'm not the only one to feel this way. Gary Lister, a school board member from Georgia, has compiled an e-book, *99 Reasons to Never, Ever Again Run for School Board*, with contributions from current and former board members from around the country.

So what if there are actually only fifty-four reasons given? (No. 4: "Education gobbledygook intrudes into your conversations."[1]) The overall point is still valid—school board service can be traumatizing.

In fact, I seem to exhibit some of the classic symptoms of post-traumatic stress disorder, including nightmares, flashbacks, and extreme distress from personal "triggers."

I can't sleep after I attend one of Darla's school events. I become agitated whenever I read an article in the paper about the district. Even worse, if I happen to bump into a current board member or an antagonist from my former days as board president, I feel an unhealthy impulse to gouge out their eyes.

You wouldn't know it from my bitter state of mind, but the only thing I ever wanted to do during my six years on the school board—six years of arguing, compromising, begging, dreaming, and, most of all, meeting—was help kids.

Of course, that's not what current board members say.

"You'll never guess what they say about you!" my last remaining friend on the board exclaims.

That I fornicated with the goats at Wilklow's (a farm next to the high school)?

Pretty much.

(No. 11: "Nothing good ever happens because of anything you did."[2])

• • •

In 1936, the first year for which reliable statistics are available, there were 118,892 school boards in the United States. Today there are 15,178. The rest have been conglomerated out of existence.[3]

Is this a good thing? It depends on your view of school boards.

If you're Anne Bryant, executive director of the National School Board Association, the vanishing school board makes you nervous. But if you're Chester E. Finn Jr., former assistant secretary of education in the Reagan administration, you don't shed many tears.[4]

"School boards are an aberration," Finn says, "an anachronism, an educational sinkhole."[5]

My own view of school boards has horribly deteriorated, like the lungs of a smoker. I started out believing that, as Bryant puts it, "in a democracy, school boards are the closest thing to the ground," a means for parents and other local taxpayers to have an impact on public education.[6] I've ended up believing kind of the opposite.

That school boards are packed with unqualified people elected by a tiny turnout of voters.

That they spend most of their time dealing with minutiae—hiring (or firing) the football coach, screening textbooks, listening to complaints about school bus stops.

That they communicate poorly, not only with administrators and each other but also with the public.

That, in the narrowness of their goals and the haphazardness of their operations, they may hinder more kids than they help.

• • •

An obvious solution would be mandatory training for all school board members. But the likelihood of that ever being implemented is about the same as the likelihood of one day discovering that Jimmy Hoffa is actually hiding out with Elvis.

Board members tend to object to mandatory training on practical rather than philosophical grounds. Many claim they haven't time for training in their already overcrowded schedules. They also say they can't spare the money for it, their own or taxpayers'.[7]

Personally, I always found that attending conferences and training sessions sponsored by the state school board association was well worth the effort. I saw new places, met new people, and learned new things.

But the current members of my local school board have other priorities. About a year ago, they voted to save a couple thousand dollars by eliminating board training from the budget.

It's ironic that those in charge of education around here would decide they can't afford to further educate themselves.

Tell me, where's the savings for the community in that?

• • •

I've another possible cure for school board dysfunction, though I'm not sure it'd be any more popular with board members than mandatory training. In fact, it may be less.

It's this—get former board members re-involved.

Every community has dozens of former board members around. They represent a vast, underutilized resource.

Even when I was serving on the board, I'd sometimes wonder why former board members never showed up at meetings. I didn't necessarily want them there hectoring us with questions and sarcastic comments, but it did strike me as odd that people who'd once been so involved in the district had so thoroughly vanished.

Probably many of them kept away because they felt like I do now, cast off and unappreciated, an orphan of local politics.

But, hell, if the United States and Vietnam can reestablish relations after thirteen ghastly years of war, then current and former board members should be able to get over their differences.

Just think of the benefits.

Former board members could serve as mentors, advisers, tribal elders. They could be organized into think tanks, kind of homey, low-key versions of the Rand Corp., to produce policy papers. They could provide history and perspective.

Or school boards could continue to flail about with all the imbecility of the Three Stooges but none of the redeeming humor.

• • •

So far I've been talking as if school boards were all of one type. They're not. School boards come in many different shapes and sizes.

Urban, suburban, and rural.

Appointed by mayors or elected by the voting public.

With as few as three members and as many as twenty-seven or more.

My local school board has seven elected members and serves a rural district, though one that's rapidly changing, like a flower in a series of time-lapse photos.

Except instead of blooming, this flower is burning.

Not only are there more students in the district than ever—about 2,000—but also more of them suffer from disabilities of one kind or another, and at a time when the federal No Child Left Behind Act has created tougher academic standards.

It's a pressure situation that the board members may not be equipped, by either background or outlook, to handle with aplomb.

• • •

Even though I probably shouldn't be, I'm surprised by just how much some of the people on the local school board resemble the typical board members described in the research literature.[8]

There's the board member with anger issues who any moment might bang his shoe on the table like Khrushchev did at the United Nations when I was a kid.

There's the micromanaging board member who wants to not only personally choose the football coach but also go out on the football field and call the plays.

There's the board member who struggled through high school and never graduated from college (about one-third of board members nationwide haven't) and now treats teachers and administrators with a kind of compensatory contempt.[9]

The whole thing reminds me somehow of one of those action-adventure movies in which, say, a plane crash-lands in the Gobi Desert. The dysfunctional board members are like the characters who become desperate and heat crazed and place their own survival above that of the group—who sneak extra drinks of precious water or plot mutiny against the natural leader.

In the movie, they'd die for their sins. In real life, they're shoo-ins for reelection.

• • •

Am I being too harsh? There may be only one way for me to find out—attend some school board meetings.

I cringe at the prospect. And can you blame me? If you'd narrowly escaped death in a cave-in, you wouldn't hurry to return underground either.

But, with a long, sad sigh, I shoulder a pick and shovel, switch on my headlamp, and descend once again into the cold darkness.

Actually, it's the high school library. The school board meets there the second and third Tuesday nights of every month.

When I was on the board, we met in the high school cafeteria, which smelled of adolescent angst, floor wax, and, depending on that day's lunch menu, perhaps Crunchy Tacos or Crispy Chicken Nuggets.

The current board apparently prefers the lofty company of books nobody takes out. Far be it from me to suggest that they ask the principal why nobody takes the books out (can't the students read yet?). I'm just there to watch.

• • •

"I don't recall who voted no for it," the vice president of the board is saying, "but it wasn't me." She sounds agitated.

The board has been plodding for at least a half hour through routine business—acknowledging correspondence and the receipt of financial reports and approving the minutes of previous meetings—when her outburst occurs.

My attention, which had drifted to the titles of the books on the library shelves, snaps back to the board table, where five members (two are missing) and the superintendent sit with hunched shoulders and serious faces in front of microphones.

"I just don't want it down in the record that it was me," she says, her voice crackling with anxiety.

Geez, I think to myself, someone needs her meds adjusted.

The superintendent, a former gym teacher who's acquired a gut since hanging up his whistle, asks, "Does anyone else remember how they voted?"

Silence.

"We're just trying to find out who voted no," he explains.

More silence.

It's then I realize all over again how grateful I should be that, after six years of board service, I've a brain that can still function above the level of a cantaloupe.

• • •

A little later, the coach of the varsity girls softball team and four of his players stand before the board. They are there to get permission for the team to go to Disney World for spring training.

The girls, who are wearing their gray practice jerseys with their numbers and nicknames in navy blue on the back, take turns outlining reasons why the trip should be allowed. The tallest of the girls, nicknamed "Sam," says, "Being together really helps team morals."

She probably means "morale," but who knows? Maybe ten days of intense exposure to Goofy does promote moral development.

The girls are clearly ill at ease addressing the board. They mumble through their parts, blushing and looking at the floor the whole time. As I listen, it strikes me that what they need isn't so much a trip to Disney as a course in public speaking, something the high school doesn't offer anymore.

When the girls finish, there are smiles and thank-yous from the board but no immediate decision on the trip. They'll be told next month, maybe.

The girls trail out of the meeting behind the coach with their heads down, disappointed and somewhat bewildered, like a team that just blew a game in the ninth inning.

• • •

"I need a motion," the board president says after reading out loud yet another turgid resolution, this one concerning that great educational controversy, the high school "boiler exhaust issue."[10]

"Move it," someone chirps.

"Second?" the president asks.

"Second," someone else says.

"All in favor?"

Five hands go up.

"Opposed?"

No hands.

"Approved," the board president says.

Were board meetings always so numbing, as if the air in the room has been laced with a powerful aerosol anesthetic? Or is it just that the people on the board now are particularly dull and futile?

Many of the items on tonight's agenda are familiar from my own days on the board—resignations, child-rearing leaves, teaching appointments, director reports. It's not exactly the stuff dreams or blue-ribbon schools are made of.

I suppose it doesn't help either that school business is often conducted in a kind of secret code. At one point during the meeting, the director of pupil personnel services, a woman of quite normal appearance, tells the board, "We'll be able to run off our PD-fives, -sevens, and -eights in the next week," and then mentions the "CSPE" and the "citation in the four-o-five."

Whatever language she's speaking, it isn't English. I'm not sure it's even human.

• • •

Things liven up considerably at about 10:00 P.M., three long hours into the meeting, when the board turns to item 7b on the agenda, "Final Discussion and Approval of the Athletic Code of Conduct for the Highland Central School District."[11]

Several months ago, word circulated through the district that varsity athletes from the fall sports teams had held a drinking party in a motel room across the river. If true, this violated a no-alcohol pledge the athletes had signed.

But, as discussed in chapter 2, the athletic director wasn't able to get the athletes to incriminate themselves or snitch on each other despite his resorting to interrogation techniques from the Spanish Inquisition. In the end, no one was punished for boozing it up (or worse) at the party.

Board members were outraged that the party animals had eluded capture. They ordered the athletic director to form a committee to revise the athletic code. It's that revision they'll approve tonight.

Only they don't.

• • •

"This just doesn't do it for me," the board president says with a frown. "I'd have to up the ante for the first offense."

You mean like sticking the heads of student athletes who smoke, drink, or use drugs on poles outside the high school?

As if reading my mind, the superintendent says, "I think the school should be about teaching kids. We shouldn't throw kids away."

The president's frown deepens. "I don't think in this area we should give second chances."

A board member who's fat and bald and best known for his mild manner says, "We asked them to form a committee to make a new policy. I don't think we should send them a mixed message and go back to the old policy." But he says this so mildly that he doesn't sound entirely convinced of it himself.

"How come there weren't people on the committee?" the vice president of the board asks. The other board members ignore her, probably because the question makes no more sense to them than it does to me.

Instead, the only other woman on the board says, "I was never really in favor of adopting a new policy. I think the old policy was strict, and I'm perfectly comfortable with that. Athletes need to be held to a higher standard."

The superintendent tries again to break the board's fixation with punishment. "Sometimes kids make mistakes," he says. "When they do, it's an opportunity to teach them."

"Why don't we give 'em polygraph tests?" the vice president suggests. "Ask 'em, 'Did you smoke a cigarette this week?'"

"It's the athletic department's failure to enforce the existing rules that's been the issue," the other woman board member says, "not the policy."

The last board member now speaks up. "I'm against the old policy and the new policy," he announces.

I glance at the superintendent. His face is a blank. He knows from past experience that the board will go round and round for the next hour and then decide not to decide anything yet.

Although I don't particularly respect or trust him—like most superintendents, he's as much a politician as an educator—I almost feel sorry for him.

• • •

Sometime after 11, the board finally adjourns its public session and enters into "exec."

I walk out of the school alone. The rest of the public—a young reporter from the local weekly—left earlier.

As I cross the parking lot and climb into my car, I can hear coyotes howling in the distance. It's an eerie and unsettling sound, like the big, gulping sobs of little children.

A part of my mind is still back at the meeting as I drive home along the dark country roads. I think about how the board president kept contradicting the superintendent and how the other board members talked in circles. But mostly I think about how students will suffer second-rate schools because the board can't seem to make decisions on matters of consequence or cooperate with the administration.

I pull up in front of my house. When I was on the board, I usually came home from meetings to find the lights out and everyone asleep. Tonight, as if in celebration of my safe return, the lights are blazing.

• • •

Some say the problem with public education isn't the school board system itself but the numerous restraints under which local school boards are forced to operate. William G. Howell, editor of the 2005 book *Besieged: School Boards and the Future of Education Politics*, points out, "Most everything that school boards do is now subject to regulations handed down from city councils, state boards of education and legislatures, the federal government, and federal courts."[12]

A prime example is the federal No Child Left Behind Act. Whether school boards think No Child Left Behind is good or bad for education is irrelevant. It's the law, and school boards must comply with its objectives or face serious sanctions.

And so we're treated to the spectacle of school boards all over the country scrambling to pay for programs and materials that promise to raise student test scores. School boards, in other words, don't get to choose what's taught in their districts. The choice has already been made for them by far-off bureaucrats.

But loss of local autonomy isn't always bad. Without federal intervention, would schools be racially desegregated even to the limited extent they are today? Would the disabled ever have achieved the right to equal education?

I doubt it, and in case you don't, just remember what the school board in Cobb County, Georgia, tried to pull in 2002. Students there would still be using biology textbooks adorned with antievolution stickers if a federal judge hadn't declared the stickers unconstitutional.[13]

There have always been and always will be various kinds of restraints—political, financial, judicial—on local school boards. But the most crippling restraints may not be the ones imposed by legislatures or courts. The most crippling may be those that board members, in the depths of their personalities, forge themselves.

• • •

Or, to put it more plainly, a person who's a jerk in other phases of his life is pretty much guaranteed to also be a jerk in his school board activities.

I saw that at the meeting. The school board president, who seems, like the Mafia, to thrive on belligerence, acted belligerently. The vice president, who's been hyperanxious ever since her divorce, acted anxiously. The fat, bald man, who's inoffensive by nature, acted inoffensively.

Throughout the meeting, the strengths and weaknesses of the various board members—but particularly their weaknesses—kept erupting into the decision-making process and blowing the presumed outcome to smithereens.

You might think that board members, whatever their quirks, hang-ups, manias, or neuroses, would rise to the responsibilities of the job, but most don't. Most bring the job down to their own level, which is somewhere dark and nasty that you really don't want to be.

During my first years on the school board, I used to read articles and books about being an effective board member.[14] The authors all said the same thing. Board members should be well informed and broad-minded and display vision, teamwork, and equanimity.

But here's the problem. School board membership generally attracts people who don't even know what equanimity is and, if they did, still wouldn't be able to display it.

• • •

A week after I attend my first school board meeting in two years, I have a strange dream.

In the dream, I arrive at the high school at about 7:00 P.M., just as the light is filtering from the sky. I get out of my car and walk to the main doors, but though a school board meeting is scheduled for that night, the doors are locked. I bang on the glass with my fist; no one comes. I then look around more closely and discover that my car is the only car in the parking lot.

Suddenly, I'm sitting in a red vinyl booth in the diner with the longest-serving board member, a building contractor who, in the dream, resembles pro wrestler cum Minnesota governor Jesse "The Body" Ventura. "Uh, yeah," he says in a slow, duncelike voice, "you missed the meeting." The board apparently did meet at the high school at 7–7 in the morning! I realize without Jesse Ventura saying it that the meeting time was moved to avoid having me there.

Dawn is still a couple hours away when I struggle awake, astonished at how extensive my paranoia has become. Then again, raging paranoia may be the only appropriate response to the fact that the local public schools have been entrusted to the cast of the World Wrestling Federation.

I try to go back to sleep but can't. It's as if my scars, invisible during the day, leap out in the dark.

● ● ●

My mother used to call me a "worrier."

"You're such a worrier," she'd always say. "You worry about everything."

She somehow made it sound like an endearing trait. It isn't necessarily, though, is it?

I know I shouldn't worry about the schools anymore. I know the education of the community's children is no longer my personal responsibility. I know I'm free now to worry instead about who's going to win on *American Idol*.

But here I am, lying wide awake next to my sleeping wife and worrying about catastrophic ignorance, government at all levels becoming a tasteless parody of democracy, coyotes roaming the town infected with rabies, murdered young minds.

In the yard, birds have begun to sing, as if they had some secret reason to be happy. I turn my head so I can see out the bedroom window.

The world is growing light.

NOTES

1. Gary Lister, *99 Reasons to Never, Ever Again Run for School Board*, http://www.nsba.org/site/page.asp? (accessed June 20, 2005).

2. Lister, *99 Reasons to Never, Ever Again Run for School Board*.

3. William G. Howell, "School Boards Besieged," *Education Week*, March 9, 2005, 32.

4. Jane Elizabeth, "School Boards' Worth in Doubt," *Pittsburgh Post-Gazette*, http://www.post-gazette.com (accessed June 21, 2005).

5. Quoted in Elizabeth, "School Boards' Worth in Doubt."

6. Quoted in Elizabeth, "School Boards' Worth in Doubt."

7. Jane Elizabeth, "School Boards Reform Elusive," *Pittsburgh Post-Gazette*, http://www.post-gazette.com (accessed June 21, 2005).

8. For a summary of the research findings, see Elizabeth, "School Boards' Worth in Doubt."

9. The statistic can be found in Elizabeth, "School Boards' Worth in Doubt."

10. Board of Education Agenda for Business Meeting, Highland (N.Y.) Central School District, July 15, 2005, 5 (photocopy).

11. Board of Education Agenda for Business Meeting.

12. Howell, "School Boards Besieged," 32.

13. Associated Press, "Judge Nixes Evolution Textbook Stickers," http://www.msnbc.msn.com/id/6822028 (accessed July 27, 2005).

14. I also wrote a few. See my *Educated Guess: A School Board Member Reflects* (Lanham, Md.: Scarecrow Education, 2003), and *Inside the Board Room: Reflections of a Former School Board Member* (Lanham, Md.: Rowman & Littlefield Education, 2006).

THE END OF SOMETHING

(Being a Chapter-by-Chapter Epilogue)

1. DOING THE MATH

We'd been notified by mail that Darla would be among the students honored one June night at an academic awards ceremony in the high school auditorium. Naturally, Barbara and I went.

Darla was called up to the stage twice, the first time to receive a certificate for academic excellence in Spanish II and the second to receive another in Math A.

For some reason, Darla's math teacher wasn't there. Mrs. Gellar, the teacher who'd banished Darla from Accelerated Math, handed her the award.

"She say anything?" I asked Darla on the ride home.

"'Congratulations.'"

A moment later, Darla added, more to herself than to me, "Now she knows I'm not stupid."

The remark struck me with the force of a bowling ball dropped from a highway overpass.

I hadn't fully realized until then the depths of Darla's pain and humiliation at having struggled in Accelerated Math and been treated by Mrs. Gellar with ill-concealed contempt. The experience had made her feel not only inadequate as a student but also unlovable as a person.

Ever since that night, I've thought that maybe kids should wear buttons or T-shirts to school imprinted with the motto, "I'm not stupid." Even if it didn't inspire teachers to love them more, it might at least serve as a daily reminder to hurt them less.

2. A SNITCH IN TIME

The kids at Darla's high school had been subjected to petty and oppressive rules all year—no halter tops, no food or drink in the classrooms (there might be vodka in that water bottle!), no driving to school without a special permit. Some of them finally went kind of nuts, like the sadistically abused prisoners in the B movie *Riot in Cellblock 11*.

They stuffed dead fish in lockers and vending machines. They superglued the doors to the school shut. They graffitied the outside bricks with speculations as to the incontinence and/or sexual depravity of district administrators.

The administrators responded the only way they seem to know how—by reprising the investigation into the drinking party at the motel. Suspects were rounded up, pummeled with accusations and questions, and ordered to confess.

This time it actually worked. About ten seniors were arrested and charged with various despicable crimes against a building. They also were banned from attending graduation. One even lost his college scholarship.

The administrators must've felt pleased.

But it's axiomatic—the greater the repression, the greater the blowback.

On the very last day of their high school careers, senior girls took off their shirts and strolled through the halls in bikini tops. Across their stomachs, they had written in marker, "What dress code?"

3. TWILIGHT'S LAST GLEAMING

Students continue to emerge from high school with all the political awareness of a coma victim. What little civics they're taught, they're taught badly. Of course, they must be learning something in class. It just isn't anything that would make them less apathetic.

Probably the best you could say about the social studies curriculum is that it's effective as a painkiller. Every year public schools turn out tens of thousands of graduates who are so numb to the larger world that they barely realize that other countries exist or have a right to.

American democracy has stalled. (Who would've guessed it had the engine of a 1973 Ford Pinto?) And we the people don't even have the sense to get out and push.

4. THOSE WHO CAN'T

Darla has been taking private voice lessons. Now her singing doesn't so much fill space with a shimmery sound as create its own space. With her firm, clear voice, she carves out of the air a sunlit room, all white and gold, a kind of sanctuary where you can meditate, marvel, or just disappear.

Will she become a teacher? She still talks like she might. And I still worry that if she does, she'll have squandered her intelligence and talent.

Her voice floats to me from somewhere in the house. I recognize the song. It's "Oh, What a Beautiful Morning."

5. BOARD TO DEATH

The chairwoman of the local Democratic committee had left a message on my machine. "I've a politically significant question to ask you," she said.

I knew what the question would be. I called her back anyway, out of politeness or maybe masochism.

"How'd you like to run for town council?" she asked.

Why not just ask me how I'd like to be trounced at the polls? A Democrat probably can get elected in my town, but a Hooters opening next door to the holiest shrine in Islam is somewhat more likely.

"The committee met last night," she went on, "and we think you'd make a great candidate. You're accomplished and respected, and you've got name recognition."

"I'm flattered," I said, and I suppose a part of me was.

She started talking about the Republican incumbents and the issues facing the town and the need for the local Democrats to field a strong team of candidates, and then she said, "Think about it, okay?"

"Okay." Actually, I'd already thought about it, and what I thought was I'd rather be fed fully conscious into a wood chipper than run for office again.

"Call me tomorrow," she said. "Don't forget."

I hung up. Tomorrow I'd call and tell her that I had other priorities.

It hadn't rained in a couple of days. Still shaking my head over our conversation, I went outside and unwound the garden hose. The flowers looked thirsty.